LAURA NELSON

The Whydah Pirates Speak

First published by Postillion LLC 2016

Copyright © 2016 by Laura Nelson

All rights reserved. No part of this publication may be reproduced, stored or transmitted in any form or by any means, electronic, mechanical, photocopying, recording, scanning, or otherwise without written permission from the publisher. It is illegal to copy this book, post it to a website, or distribute it by any other means without permission.

Laura Nelson asserts the moral right to be identified as the author of this work.

Laura Nelson has no responsibility for the persistence or accuracy of URLs for external or third-party Internet Websites referred to in this publication and does not guarantee that any content on such Websites is, or will remain, accurate or appropriate.

Designations used by companies to distinguish their products are often claimed as trademarks. All brand names and product names used in this book and on its cover are trade names, service marks, trademarks and registered trademarks of their respective owners. The publishers and the book are not associated with any product or vendor mentioned in this book. None of the companies referenced within the book have endorsed the book.

Second edition

ISBN: 978-0692737958

This book was professionally typeset on Reedsy.
Find out more at reedsy.com

Dedicated to the pirates of the Whydah and her escorts, some who survived, some who perished in the storm, the prisoners who had no choice, and some French pirates who went their separate ways to their separate fates.

Contents

Acknowledgement	ii
Peter Cornelius Hoof and Me	1
John Julian - The Teenage Pirate	18
The Unknown Survivor	24
Sam Bellamy & Olivier Levasseur – Two Pirates Just Kickin'...	29
John King – The Boy Pirate	37
The Trials of Eight Persons Indited for Piracy	42
The Trial of Thomas Davis	65
Instructions to the Living, From the Condition of the Dead	79
Warnings to Them that make Haste to be Rich	99
Appendix	110
Bibliography	117
Index	120
Notes	126
About the Author	132
Also by Laura Nelson	133

Acknowledgement

Original cover art and design by Suzanne Sudekum of Sudekum Design.

Transcripts of "The Trials of Eight Persons" and "Instructions to the Living" courtesy of Evans Early American Imprint Collection.

All articles have been edited and corrections made since their original publication.

Peter Cornelius Hoof and Me

My interest in Peter Cornelius Hoof began when I attended the Real Pirates Exhibit in Denver, Colorado, in June 2011.[1] Like many people, I found the exhibit fascinating and came away with two books and what I thought, at the time, was a new interest in pirates. While reading these books, I became conscious of Peter Hoof and began to have an interest in him. Why his name leaped out at me from the pages of these books, I do not know. I may never know. All I know is that it happened, and my life has been enriched ever since.

At one point in the exhibit, there was a display where visitors could touch coins from the wreck of the *Whydah*. While touching them, I felt a whooshing sensation and a drain of energy. I put it down to having been in the exhibit for a long time with no food or water. I just figured I must be really hungry and, once I got something to eat, I would be better.

During the next month, I did a lot of research on pirates. They were a new obsession. Not only was I doing a lot of research, I wrote about them, too! I had done some writing while in college but following graduation I never seemed to write for more than a paragraph or two. After attending the exhibit, my dreams involved sequences of events surrounding pirates. When I wrote down the most recent changes, the vents in the dreams moved forward. Neither the writing nor the dreams were sequential. There was, however, one common theme: a pirate with brown hair and eyes, who either sought me out or appeared out of nowhere to protect me from a dangerous situation.

A month after my first visit, I returned to the exhibit. The second visit was in some ways more amazing than the first. When I approached the coin display, I discovered that, conveniently, no one else was around. I closed my eyes, took a deep breath, and asked if I had a connection to the wreck. I touched all the coins, one or two at a time. Toward the end, a voice told me that I was not on the *Whydah*, but that I lost a lover in the wreck.[2] Then I experienced the same whooshing sensation and drain of energy I had felt the first time I touched the coins.

About a month after my second visit to the exhibit, I chanced to run across a medium who did past life regression at a county fair in Denver. I told her what had been happening to me, and she confirmed I was not a pirate myself, but that I did know many of them. Several members of my immediate family left with the pirates, which angered me because I was a female in that past life and thus could not go with them.

During a second session with the medium In December 2011, Peter asked me to tell his story. His soul was stuck and telling his story would help him to move forward and go on. So, I told his story to several people, but had a feeling while doing so that this was not the way to go. One friend said that even if it wasn't a best seller, I had to get his story out there. On that day, the idea for this article was born. Peter was not a captain among the pirates, but he was hanged for piracy, and for that reason his name is recorded in the record books.

As part of his interrogation before his trial, on 6 May 1717, Peter stated:

"That he was born in Sweden, is about 34 years old, and left his Country 18 Years ago. He Sail'd for the most part with the Dutch on the coast of Portobello, and has been with the Pirates fourteen Months. When he was taken by Bellamy in a Periaga, he belong'd to a Ship whereof one Cornelison was Master...[3]

At the time Peter was taken captive, Samuel Bellamy still sailed with a pirate named Benjamin Hornigold, who sailed in consort with the French pirate, Louie Labous (also known as Olivier Levasseur or La Buse). La Buse got the nickname of "The Buzzard" for the swift and merciless was he had of attacking his victims.

Peter was "among the most prized of the new recruits."[4] His previous seventeen years of sailing along the Spanish Main provided him with extensive knowledge of the southern Caribbean, and greatly added to the pirate's navigational knowledge.

A lot of you are familiar with how pirates in the Golden Age took captives. They came upon a boat swiftly and used methods calculated to instill the maximum amount of fear in their targets. Imagine the scene: A large number of armed, screaming pirates come pouring over the side of your vessel after firing a shot across the bow of the ship. The captain of your ship has only put up a paltry defense and stopped his ship based on the theory that giving in to the pirates will prevent them from doing any more damage than is necessary to passengers and crew. You are forced into a corner and made to kneel to reduce the chance of you retaliating.

Sailors in these days were poorly paid, some as little as a few shillings a month, so you have next to no personal possessions to speak of. Now the little that you own is in jeopardy of being taken away by the pirates.

Then the captain of your vessel is forced to relate the skills and marital status of each member of the crew. Some volunteer to join the pirates, wanting a life of lawlessness and plundering.

But not all go willingly. You are forced to accompany the pirates because of your knowledge and experience. You do not wish to join them, but your feelings in the matter are not considered. On the pirate vessel you are considered a prisoner. All the status you spent your life working for is now gone. These people are not your friends. You have left behind the life you knew and the friends you made.

That night, you are lifted to your feet, blindfolded, and marched to you know not where. When the blindfold is torn off, you face a sort of tribunal of the most senior of the pirates. Keep in mind that on the old sailing vessels the areas below decks were poorly lit, so you cannot see well.

You face this tribunal alone. They sit behind a table. The rest of the pirates are amassed behind you, so there is no escape. If you refuse to sign the articles, you will be shot, and your body will be summarily disposed of on the sea. So, you sign, because you wish to live and have no alternative. After you sign, you realize that your life as you have known it is over and you feel as though you have made a deal with the devil.

During interrogation before their trial in Boston, Massachusetts, one of the *Whydah* pirates, John Brown, testified that Peter "was once whip'd for attempting to Run-away..."[5] In his examination, Simon Van Vorst relates that while on the island of St. Croix, "3 of their Men Ran away, and one of them being brought back was severely whipped."[6] But he did not give specific names.

The impression I got from Peter was that he felt this was his last chance to escape the pirates and return to his normal life. I also got the impression that at the "advanced" age of thirty-four, he wanted to return to a relationship with someone he had met in the past.

Flogging (whipping) in Peter's time was done with a cat-o'-nine tails, a device with a handle and nine ropes, usually with a piece of lead at the end of each one to tear the skin. All descriptions I have seen of this punishment describe it as being excruciatingly painful.

During my next session with the medium, Peter described some of the ordeal: "After they were through whipping me, I could not move on my own. I slumped to the deck, helpless, tears streaming from my eyes, my throat raw from screaming, my body shaking uncontrollably with the pain. Eventually, someone took pity on me and picked me up, taking me to a dark quiet place where I was lucky there was a doctor on board who cared enough to clean and stitch me up. My hands continued trembling for a long time; the pain is tremendous. I laid there nearly unmoving for three days. I had to be helped to the head and brought food. It was agony to eat. Eventually I was able to move on my own again, slowly at first, to keep the wounds from opening. I was lucky and my wounds did not become infected."

According to Thomas Trotter's observations of flogging victims, "such whipped patients were so psychologically disturbed that they frequently went into fits of hysteria, weeping, and delirium, while the other men in the wards silently looked on and wept in sympathy, and finally turned their heads away."[7]

Peter told me that he eventually became a pirate, but he did not torture or beat any prisoners or captives and did not approve of the pirates' treatment of women. The lesson he wished for me to take away from his experience was that you can do something bad, but not necessarily participate in every aspect of the bad thing.

Some pirate historians doubt that men were pressed into serving on pirate ships. Some insist they only pretended to be forced to hide the fact that they wanted to go with the pirates and share in the booty and freedom of the pirate lifestyle. Claiming to have been pressed was a common plea by those accused of piracy at their trials. During his interrogation, Peter stated that "no married men were forced,"[8] which to me means that some men must have been pressed, otherwise why be concerned about whether a man was married? Unfortunately, the transcript gives only his responses, and not what the actual questions were. Also, the interrogations were written down after the fact.

In further defense of the idea that men were pressed into piracy, John Brown said, "there were about 50 Men forced, over whom the Pirates kept a watchful eye…" He then goes on to say that "the names of the forced Men were put in the watch Bill and fared as others"; meaning they were on the ship's duty roster and did the same shipboard tasks as the pirates.[9]

But consider the situation: you have a person, forcibly taken from his job and his friends. He is threatened with death if he does not "sign on" as a pirate and bullied and belittled by nearly everyone aboard. Peter testified during the trial, "Bellamy's Company Swore they would kill him unless he would joyn with them in their Unlawful designs."[10]

When Peter was taken captive, Sam Bellamy was sailing as a member of Benjamin Hornigold's crew. Bellamy had joined Hornigold to learn the ropes of piracy. At the time of Peter's capture, Samuel Bellamy had taken it upon himself to attack Peter's ship while Hornigold was away getting supplies.

Three weeks after Peter was taken, a difference arose amongst Hornigold's crew about whether to attack English ships. Hornigold did not wish to attack them, but Bellamy and others felt they were missing out on too many potentially lucrative targets. Following pirate tradition, the entire crew voted. Samuel Bellamy was elected captain and sailed away with half of the crew and some captives. Hornigold went his own way with the dissenting pirates, including a man named Edward Teach, who would later become known as Blackbeard.

Bellamy and his crew of pirates traveled through Baya Honda, Cape Corrientes, and the Isle of Pines, then around to the eastern tip of Cuba. From June to August 1716, they were on the north coast of what is now Haiti. In September, they were in the area of present-day Puerto Rico. In October, they sailed from Samana Bay to Cape Nicholas, Hispaniola.

Around November or December 1716, Bellamy captured a galley called *Sultana* in the vicinity of St. Croix. With a few "piractical" alterations, he made her his new flagship. In January 1717, La Buse and his crew decided to leave Bellamy's company and head in another direction. Their parting was friendly.

Early in March, Samuel Bellamy was made aware of, either by unknown sources or by spotting, the *Whydah*, which was setting out on her return voyage to England after making the trip from Africa and the Caribbean (the "Middle Passage") to buy and sell slaves. Bellamy, who was seeking a "Ship of Force" so he could take larger prizes, pursued her.[11] Peter's extensive knowledge of the South Caribbean was instrumental to the success of this pursuit, which last three days.

Once they caught up to the *Whydah*, Bellamy only had to fire one or two shots across her bow to make Captain Lawrence Prince surrender. After taking over the ship, Bellamy allowed Captain Prince and some of his men who did not wish to become pirates to sail away in the *Sultana* with a few provisions and some silver and gold. After taking a few days to re-fit the *Whydah* to suit the purposes of pirating, Bellamy continued sailing, turning towards the east coast of America.

Around 9:00am on 26 April 1717, Bellamy and his crew captured a ship called the *Mary Anne*. Seven names, including Peter's, were read off the watch bill and these were the men sent to board the prize. Five were armed with pistols and cutlasses. They took charge of the ship while sending five of her crew and captain to the *Whydah* to show Captain Bellamy their papers and be held as prisoners. The remaining crew members were kept on board the *Mary Anne* to help sail the ship.

The pirates soon learned that her hold was loaded with casks of Madeira, however the hatch was covered with heavy cables, making it too difficult for them to get into right then. The pirates had to content themselves with some wine they found in the cabins. A second small boat came over from the *Whydah* to get some wine to take back there. They also took some of the crew's clothes.

Around 3pm, fog started to settle around the flotilla. This, in addition to being drunk, caused the pirates to have trouble following Bellamy's order to follow the *Whydah* and keep the vessels together. During the evening, as the weather deteriorated, seven of the eight pirates aboard the *Mary Anne* worked on moving the cables off of the hatch to get at the Madeira in the hold. Once inside, they broke open the first barrels while taking turns at the helm.

Realizing the *Mary Anne* was falling behind, Bellamy slacked off long enough to allow them to catch up. He yelled at the pirates to "make more haste." In response, John Brown swore he would make the vessel "carry Sail till she carried her Masts away."[12]

The pirates then ordered their captives to help handle the sails and man the pumps, because the hull of the *Mary Anne* was leaking. By the time darkness fell, the helm was completely turned over to one captive, Thomas Fitzgerald. The storm was in full force by 10:00pm. Twenty to thirty-foot seas battered the *Mary Anne*. Eventually they lost sight of the Whydah, and found themselves among the breakers where the ship ran aground.

At this point, one or several of the pirates (unnamed), cried out, "For God's sake let us go down into the Hould & Die together."[13] The pirates and their captives spent the night in the hold. Thomas Fitzgerald, in response to a request from the pirates, read from the "Common-Prayer Book, which he did about an Hour…."[14]

On the morning of 27 April 1717, the men found that one side of the ship was on dry land and they could walk on to what proved to be an island without having to get their feet wet. They broke open a chest and ate sweetmeats (sugared fruits) and other food they found and drank more wine. A local named John Cole spotted them and, mistaking them for shipwrecked mariners, came across in a canoe to bring them ashore just outside Eastham, Massachusetts.[15]

According to local folklore, while at Cole's house, Peter gazed out the south window of the great room and saw men approaching the house. This posse was led by Cole's son, who had snuck out of the house to inform the authorities about the pirates. Justice of the Peace Joseph Doane finally went with him to check out the situation.

Barnstable Gaol as it appears today. Courtesy Richard Caspole of Historical Imaging.

The pirates fled but stopped at a tavern in Eastham. Legend says that Mr. Doane and the posse caught up to them at the tavern. He used liquor to loosen the pirates' tongues. Later both the posse and the pirates went to sleep in the taproom. During the night, the pirates woke up and snuck out of the tavern.

Continuing to stick together, they struck out for Rhode Island, which was known to shelter pirates. Before noon, the posse overtook them. Altogether, nine men were taken by horseback to Boston under heavy guard: Peter, Simon Van Vorst, John Brown, Hendrick Quintor, John Shuan, Thomas South, Thomas Baker, Thomas Davis, and John Julian. Of the nine, Davis would be tried separately for piracy and found not guilty. Julian, a Miskito Indian, would disappear from history.

There is some speculation he was sold into slavery. The men remained in Boston's hot, foul prison until Friday, 18 October 1717, when they were led into the Admiralty Court. They wore the same clothes they had worn the night of the shipwreck.

Map showing location of Boston Gaol. Public domain.

Of being in prison, Peter said there was never enough food or water. He was always thirsty and hungry. There were long hours of nothing to do but sit and think – think about how he would like to see his family again and how he had disappointed his father and broken his mother's heart. He thought of the sorrow he was causing them, how he should have returned to his family, and what he wouldn't give to hug his mother again and hear her voice.

On 5 September 1717, unknown to the incarcerated pirates, King George I issued a royal proclamation for the suppression of piracy that included a pardon.

...we do hereby promise, and declare, that in case of the said Pyrates, shall, on or before the Fifth Day of September, in the Year of our Lord One Thousand Seven Hundred and Eighteen, surrender him or themselves, to one of our Principal Secretaries of State in Great Britain or Ireland, or to any Governor or Deputy Governor of any of our Plantations beyond the Seas; every such Pyrate and Pyrates so surrendering him, or themselves, as foresaid, shall have our gracious Pardon...[16]

This is important to note, because there is some debate as to when exactly the authorities in Boston became aware of the pardon. There is some speculation that they knew the arrival of the pardon was imminent and thus hastened the trial and execution before it did. "The proclamation was sent out to the governors in the West Indies and the American colonies, who then had the responsibility of contacting the pirates."[17] On 9 December 1717, the Boston News-Letter published the proclamation. The *Whydah* pirates had been tried and convicted in October.

While the pirates awaited their trial, the Reverend Cotton Mather ministered to them. The eight pirates from the *Mary Anne* were about the third group of pirates he had ministered to since the famous Salem witch trials of 1690. At one point during the course of these discussions, Mather noted in his diary, "Obtain a reprieve and, if it may be, a pardon for one [of the] Pyrates, who is not only more penitent, but also more innocent than the rest."[18] Unfortunately, inquiries into historical records in Boston failed to unearth any evidence that Mather ever took and official steps towards obtaining such a pardon, nor for which specific pirate he meant to do so.

Peter says that during one of his sessions, the Reverend Mather wrote a letter to Peter's parents for him. He told them how sorry he was for hurting them so much. He also apologized for being a bad son and for not being more dutiful to them.

During his interrogation before trial, Peter gave exact information about the treasure aboard the *Whydah*:

"The money taken in the Whido, which was reported to Amount to 2000 or 3000 Pounds, was counted over in the Cabin, and put up in bags, Fifty pounds to every Man's share, there being 180 Men on Board... Their Money was kept in Chests between Decks without any guard, but none was to take any without the Quarter Master's leave."[19]

Tried alongside Peter were Simon van Vorst, John Brown, Hendrick Quintor, John Shuan, Thomas South, and Thomas Baker. It was time for them to face the court, and what a court they faced!

His Excellency Samuel Shute Esq: Governour;

Vice Admiral, & President the Honourable William Dummer Esq;

Lieutenant Governour The Honourable Elisha Hutchinson, Penn Townsend, Andrew Belcher, Hon Cushing, Nathaniel Norden, John Wheelwright, Benjamin Lynde, Thomas Hutchinson, and Thomas Fitch, Esqrs; of His Majesty's Council for this Province;

John Meinzies Esq: Judge of the Vice Admiralty; and

Capt. Thomas Smart, Commander of His majesty's Ship of War the Squirrel, and John Jekyll Esq; Collector of the Plantation Duties. (Trial, 299)

The indictment "for Crimes of Piracy, Robbery & Felony committed on the High Sea" included several articles. First, the pirates "without lawful Cause or Warrant, in Hostile manner with Force & Arms, Piractically & Feloniously did Surprize, Assault, Invade, and Enter... the *Mary Anne* of Dublin...."[20] Second, they did "Piractically & feloniously seize and imprison Andrew Crumpstey Master thereof...." Third, they did "Piractically & Feloniously Imbezil, Spoil, and Rob the cargoe of said Vessel...." And fourth, they "over powered and subdued the said Master and his Crew, and made themselves Masters of the said vessel... did then and there Piractically & Feloniously Steer and Direct their course after the above-named Piratical Ship, the *Whido*, intending to joyn and accompany the same; and thereby, to enable themselves better to pursue and accomplish their Execrable designs to oppress the Innocent, and cover the Seas with Depredations and Robberies."[21]

After reading the indictments, the court declared "all and each of them ought to be punished by Sentences of the said Court with the pain of Death, and loss of Lands, Goods and Chattels, according to the direction of the Law, and for an Example and Terror to all others."[22]

At this point in the trial, Simon Van Vorst asked for counsel for the pirates "that so they might be well advised on what to do."[23] His request was granted, and one attorney, Robert Auchmuty, was appointed to defend all seven of the pirates, but after two of his motions were denied, he resigned.[24] One of those motions was to allow Thomas Davis, a carpenter on the *Whydah*, to be brought in to give evidence on the pirates' behalf. The motion was rejected because Davis was also in prison for the same offense and his guilt or innocence had not yet been determined. So, the illiterate pirates were left to face the court alone.

They all pleaded not guilty to the charges. They were given copies of the indictment and about two days to prepare for their trial. Weakened after months of confinement in a dark cell and a bread-and-water diet and compelled to stand during these proceedings, you can imagine how hard it was for any of the pirates to understand what the Advocate General was saying, much less what all of it meant. Mostly they understood that the entire proceedings were set heavily against them and they were in serious trouble.

During the trial, Peter declared in his defense that "He was taken by Capt. Bellamy in a vessel whereof John Cornelison was Master, That the said Bellamy's company Swore they would kill him unless he would joyn with them in their Unlawful Designs."[25]

An interesting part of reading the trial transcripts is that the prosecutor and witnesses have statements of one or more paragraphs, while the pirates' statements are sometimes only a sentence or two long. Obviously not much care was taken to record what each one actually said in his defense, an obvious bias by today's standards.

During their imprisonment, Blackbeard vowed to come to Boston to rescue them and did set out towards Boston from the West Indies. But before he had gone far or had even left the harbor (depending on what source you read), he found out the authorities in Boston had blockaded the harbor with a man-of-war and several other ships. This represented way too much firepower for a pirate ship, so Blackbeard abandoned the rescue attempt. After the six pirates were hanged, he took out his vengeance on several ships from Boston, burning them to the waterline, cargo and all, a specific example being a ship called the *Protestant Caesar*, in the Bay of Honduras.

Although Peter's trial was completed on 18 October, he and the other pirates were not hanged until 15 November 1717. All of them, except Thomas South, were found guilty of the crimes of piracy, robbery and felony on the High Seas. They were sentenced to be hanged until dead. South was the only one whose plea of being a forced man was believed by the court and was found not guilty.

In 1717 hanging was not like you see in the Wild West movies where the noose is tied around the neck, a horse or wagon is kicked out from underneath the victim, his neck snaps from the force of the drop and, in a couple of minutes, he is dead. Hanging at this time was done by a method called the short drop. The noose is tied around the neck, but the body is only dropped short distance, not enough to break the neck. What killed the person was the slow movement of the noose against the neck, causing a prolonged, torturous death by slow asphyxiation. The entire process took about fifteen to twenty minutes, during which time the body naturally struggled to breathe.

Hangings were a public event, attended by hordes of people, who jeered and taunted the victims. Even children were brought along to watch the victims choke to death. To get to the scaffold, the pirates walked through town to a canoe, where they were then rowed across to the mudflats at the Charlestown ferry landing to be hanged.

Cotton Mather accompanied them to the place of execution. Unfortunately, he did not record all of the conversations he had with the eight men during their e=several months of confinement. Aside from their interrogations before trial, Mather only published his final conversations with them as they walked to the gallows. To add yet another unfortunate aspect to the lack of historical documents, he only wrote down these conversations after the hangings were concluded. He apparently was not accompanied by any sort of secretary or scribe to record the conversations as they happened. So their content must be seen through the filter of Mather's recollection.

He recorded his final conversation with Peter thusly:

CM: Hoof, A melted Heart would now be a comfortable Symptom upon thee. Do you find anything of it?

PH: Something of it; I wish it were more!

CM: To pursue the Good Intention, I will now give a Blow with an hammer, that breaks the Rocks to pieces. I will bring you the most Heart-melting Word, as ever was heard in the World. We find in the Sacred Scripture such a word as this; CHRIST, who is GOD, does beseech you. Be ye Reconciled unto GOD. That ever the Son of GOD should come to us, with such a Message from His Eternal Father! What? After we have so Offended His Infinite Majesty! After we have been so Vile, so Vile – and He stands in so little Need of us? To beseech such Criminals, to be Reconciled unto the Holy GOD, and be willing to be Happy in His Favour! O Wonderful! Wonderful! Methinks, it cannot be heard without flowing Tears of Joy!

PH: Ah! But what shall I do to be Reconciled unto GOD!

CM: Make an Answer, make an Echo, unto this Wonderful World of your SAVIOUR. And what can you make but this? – And for this also, you must have the Help of His Grace to make it; O my dear SAVIOUR, I beseech thee to Reconcile me unto GOD.

PH: Oh! That it might be so!

CM: A Reconciliation to GOD is the only thing you have now to be concern'd about. If this be not accomplished before a few minutes more are Expired, you go into the Strange Punishment reserved for the Workers of Iniquity. You go, where He that made you, will not have Mercy on you; He that formed you, will shew you no favour. But it is not yet altogether Too Late. An Hearty Consent unto the Motions of the Reconciler, will prepare you to pass from an Ignominious Death, into [an] Inconceivable Glory.

PH: Oh! Let me hear them!

CM: First, You must Consent unto This; O my SAVIOUR, I fly to thy Sacrifice, I beg, I beg, that for the sake of That, they Wrath may be turned away from me; I cannot bear to have they Wrath Lying on me! Can you say so?

PH: I say it, I say it!

CM: But then, you must Consent unto This also; O my SAVIOUR, I Cry unto thee, to take away all that is contrary to GOD in my Soul; and cause me to Love God with all my Soul; and Conquer my depraved Will; and bring to Right all that is Wrong in my Affections; and let my Will become entirely subject unto the Will of GOD in all things. Can you say so.

PH: I say it, I say it!

CM: If it be heartily said, The Reconciliation is accomplished. But if you were to Live your Life over again, how would you Live it?

PH: Not as I have done!

CM: How then?

PH: In serving of GOD, and in doing of Good unto Men.

CM: God Accept you. Oh! That you SAVIOUR might now say to you as He said in a Dying Hour, unto One, who died as a Thief, This Day thou shalt be with me in Paradise. I do with some Encouragement leave you in His Glorious Hands.

PH: O my dear JESUS! I lay hold on thee; and I resolve, never, never, to let thee go!

CM: May he help you to keep your hold, of the Hope set before you.

PH: My death this Afternoon is nothing, 'tis nothing; 'Tis the wrath of a terrible GOD after Death abiding on me, which is all that I am afraid of.

CM: There is JESUS, who delivers from the Wrath to come; With Him I leave you. (Mather, Instructions, 138 – 139)

On the scaffold, awaiting their hanging, Peter and Thomas Baker appeared "very distinguishingly Penitent."[26] Nothing else is said about the appearance of the other pirates. John Brown gave a speech in "too much of the Language he had been used unto."[27]

No death certificate exists for Peter. Lacking burial records, modern researchers believe that after the pirates were hanged, their bodies were subsequently covered in tar and hung in gibbets near the harbor to rot and serve as a warnings to sailors against becoming pirates. Absent other evidence, this would seem to have been the fate of the *Whydah* pirates.

Unfortunately, because of centuries of "wharfing out," the filling in and building up of land to extend the city farther into the harbor, it is no longer possible to walk the same ground that Peter did in 1717, as that ground simply no longer exists. The jail where he was held is long gone. The Old State House, where the trial was held, used to be almost at the harbor, but is now in the middle of downtown Boston (again because of the wharfing out process.) The building itself only vaguely resembles its original design. It has been re-purposed, restored, and re-built several times over the ensuing centuries. For example, the last time it was "re-worked," the architect installed a spiral staircase, which is not authentic to the building as the original design did not have one. Early in the 1900s the basement of the Old State House was excavated and turned into a subway stop now appropriately called the State stop. It took public outcry to bring in legislation to prevent further commercialization of the building.

While visiting Boston, I made a trip to Provincetown, on Cape Cod, to visit the Whydah Pirate Museum. There I was able to see even more artifacts of the wreck of the *Whydah*. I was able to touch more coins, some ballast stones, a cannon round, and a bar shot. And yes, I got the same energy drain that I experienced during the traveling Real Pirates exhibit. In fact, I almost fell over!

Through all of this, Peter has been a wonderful person to work with. He was a happy-go-lucky person before the pirates took him captive. He still has a wonderful sense of humor. He also has the manners of a gentleman, even though the class restrictions of his day prevented him from being one. This ability to walk in both worlds, the world of manners and the world of the pirates, allowed him to survive and function among the pirates. I hope that writing this article will help his soul to move forward as he hoped.

The lesson I wish for you to take away from this is that any one of us, even someone who considers himself or herself to be a nice person, as Peter did, can make a poor choice or a bad decision. In Peter's case, his choices and decisions put him into a situation that he could not readily get out of. It can happen to anyone.

"Peter Cornelius Hoof and Me" originally published in April and May of

2013 in the online newsletter *Pirates and Privateers* on the website *Thistles and Pirates* and also on the *History is Now* web site.

John Julian - The Teenage Pirate

There are only two known survivors of the April 1717 wreck of the *Whydah* commanded by Sam Bellamy. Thomas Davis, a carpenter, and John Julian, a pilot.[28] Although the majority of historical records list John as a Cape Cod Indian, further research by the team recovering artifacts from the wreck site reveals that he was actually a Miskito Indian from the region of Nicaragua and Honduras in Central America called the Costa de Miskitos (the Mosquito Coast.)

"John was probably around 16 year old when he became the Whydah's pilot and guided it in and out of hidden harbors through the difficult waters of Cape Cod."[29]

According to William Dampier, who interacted with the Miskito Indians circa 1687, "They are tall, well made, raw-boned, lusty, strong, and nimble of foot; long visage, lank black hair, look stern, hard favour'd, and of a dark Copper-colour Complexion.... Their chiefest employment in their own Country is to strike Fish, Turtle, or Manatee.... For this they are esteemed by all Privateers; for one or two of them in a Ship will maintain 100 men; So that when we careen our Ships, we choose commonly such places where there is plenty of Turtle or Manatee for these *Moskito* Men to strike and it is very rare to find Privateers destitute of one or more of them, when the Commander, or most of the Men are *English*...."[30]

In addition to their fishing skills, Dampier also wrote, "They are very ingenious at throwing the Lance, Fisgig, Harpoon, or any manner of Dart.[31] He then goes on to comment that "...they often come with the Seamen."[32]

Colin Woodard in his book *The Republic of Pirates* states that John "had served with Bellamy aboard his periaguas.[33] While there is no specific record of how John joined Bellamy's crew, in March 1715, Bellamy was with a band of pirates that operated in the Bay of Honduras, the region where the Miskito Indians lived.

It was common that when a pirate crew captured a slave ship still carrying its cargo, many slaves, once freed, joined the pirates.[34] Even if they lacked skills as seamen, they often had martial skills that made them valuable to their new crews. Many learned sailing skills after joining the pirates.

"Blacks received shares of booty and enjoyed other perquisites of crew membership, including the right to vote. Rewards and incentives appear to have been based on an individual's ability to function effectively within the pirate crew rather than on skin color."[35]

Black men were well represented among pirate crews:

Blackbeard's crew was 60 percent black;

Edward England's crew of 300 included about 80 black pirates;

Half of John Lewis's crew of 80 were black men from English colonies;

On his last voyage, Christopher Condent's crew of some 500 pirates included an estimated 200 black men;*

Bart Roberts's crew included 70 black men out of a total of 267; and

Two pirate crews, the names of their commanders unknown, were almost 100 percent black. (Clifford, Real, 80)

According to *A General History of the Pyrates*, when Captain Olivier Levasseur (also known as La Buse, the Buzzard) met up with Howell Davis off the coast of Gambia, half of his crew were blacks.

While sailing with Samuel Bellamy, John Julian may have traveled to such places as the Gulf of Cuba; Honduras; Portobello in Panama; Baya Honda, Cuba; Cape Corrientes and the Isle of Pines in Puerto Rico; the north coast of Haiti; St. Croix; and La Isla Blanquilla in Venezuela. Along the way he participated in capturing and plundering ships and experienced what it meant to dress in fine clothes and have a pocket full of money. He also rose to the position of pilot, making him responsible for guiding the pirate ships in and out of hidden harbors to escape the authorities.

April 26, 1717, started out like any other day for the pirates. In the morning, they captured the *Mary Anne*, "a pink with more than 7,000 gallons of Madeira on board... and the *Fisher* – a small sloop with a cargo of deer hides and tobacco, captured that afternoon."[36] John remained on board the *Whydah* that day, having not been sent over to the *Fisher* or the *Mary Anne* as part of their prize crews.

In the evening a storm began to roll in, heralded by a dense fog.[37] "According to eyewitness accounts, gusts topped 70 miles [113 kilometers] an hour and the seas rose to 30 feet [9 meters].[38] The accident was best expressed by Thomas Davis in his deposition before his trial:

The Ship being at an Anchor, they cut their Cables and ran a shoar; in a quarter of an hour after the Ship struck, the Main-mast was carried by the board, and in the Morning She was beat to pieces. About Sixteen Prisoners drown'd; Crumpstey, Master of the Pink being one, and One hundred and forty-four in all.[39]

"Although the beach was just 500 feet away, the bitter ocean temperatures were cold enough to kill the strongest swimmer within minutes. Other crew members were crushed by the weight of falling rigging, cannon, and cargo as the ship, her treasure, and the remaining men on board plunged to the ocean floor, swallowed up by the shifting sands of the cape."[40]

When locals arrived on the shore the next morning "more than a hundred mutilated corpses lay at the wrack line with the ship's timbers."[41]

Yet somehow John Julian and Thomas Davis managed to reach the shore, and then climb the steep, seventy foot sand cliffs of what is now called Marconi Beach. While Davis found temporary refuge in the home of Cape Cod locals Samuel Harding and his wife, "There is no historical record telling where John was."[42] John suddenly reappears as part of a group of nine pirates who were arrested and taken on horseback to Boston Gaol a day or so after the wreck. The other eight pirates included Thomas Davis and the survivors from the prize ship *Mary Anne*: Hendrick Quintor, Thomas South, Peter Cornelius Hoof, John Shuan, John Brown, Thomas Baker, and Simon Van Vorst. (South and Davis would be acquitted of piracy.)

But unlike his comrades, John did not stand trial for piracy. According to National Geographic's "Pirates of the Whydah," "he was probably the Julian the Indian bought by John Quincy – whose grandson, President John Quincy

Adams, became a staunch abolitionist."[43]

If John Julian and Julian the Indian were the same person, he suffered. "A purportedly 'unruly slave,' Julian the Indian was sold to another owner and tried often to escape. During one attempt he killed a bounty hunter who was trying to catch him.[44]

The Massachusetts Historical Society's website has an online presentation entitled "African Americans and the End of Slavery in Massachusetts." One article, "The Lives of Individual African Americans before 1783," notes that:

Slaves in Massachusetts usually lived with their owners and had more direct contact with family members than the way of life we associate with plantation slavery in the West Indies and later in the American south. The Massachusetts courts recognized the right of slaves to hold and dispose of some property, to keep wages for work done not on their master's time, to bring suit in court, and the right to jury trials, legal counsel, and some legal protection…

Daily life of African Americans was controlled through legislation. A 1703 law forbade blacks, Native Americans, and mulattos from venturing out after 9:00pm, unless on a master's errand… "Unruly" slaves could be punished by the law…[45]

John Quincy House - Birthplace of President John Quincy Adams on left, birthplace of President John Adams on right. Built in 1681, Quincy, Massachusetts. Courtesy Robinson Genealogical Society, Robinson Family Genealogical and Historical Association, 1912.

Ultimately, the law did catch up to John. A pithy paragraph in *The Weekly Rehearsal*, a Boston newspaper published in March 1733, says:

"Thursday next is the Day appointed for the Execution of Julian the Indian. He went Yesterday both Forenoon and Afternoon to hear the Rev. Mr. Checkley, who had prepared two Discourses suitable to the Occasion. The Rev. Ministers of the Town have taken a great deal of Pains with the unhappy Criminal, to prepare him for his approaching Change, and 'tis hoped their Labours have not been in vain."

Elizabeth Moisan, in *Master of the Sweet Trade*, wrote, "It was common for the unclaimed bodies of executed prisoners to be given to medical students for dissection, and according to an article in *The Boston Newsletter*, on March 31, 1733, John's corpse was used for this purpose. The article goes on to tell us that, 'The Bones are preserv'd in order to be fram'd into a Skeleton.' "[46] A sad end for such a young man.

"John Julian – The Teenage Pirate" originally published in October of 2013 in the online newsletter *Pirates and Privateers* on the website *Thistles and Pirates*.

*In his blog, *A Writer's Hiding Place*, Baylus Brooks reveals research that determines that the real name of this pirate was Edward Congdon. https://bcbrooks.blogspot.com/search?q=Condent

The Unknown Survivor

There are only two known survivors of the wreck of the *Whydah Galley*, commanded by Sam Bellamy: Thomas Davis, a carpenter, and John Julian, a pilot. But were they the only two men to survive the wreck?

Bellamy and his crew were sailing north along the east coast of what is now the United States. Folklore says their intended destination was Eastham in Cape Cod, Massachusetts, where Samuel Bellamy intended to pick up Maria Hallett, believed to be his lover, on their way to Rhode Island or Maine. He may also have been hoping to sell some of their booty.

April 26, 1717, started out like any other day for the pirates. In the morning, they captured the *Mary Anne*, "a pink with more than 7,000 gallons of Madeira wine on board… and then the *Fisher* – a small sloop with a cargo of deer hides and tobacco" in the afternoon.[47] Per customary pirate procedure, smaller groups of pirates were sent over to these ships from the *Whydah* to act as the new crews of their "prizes."

At the time of the wreck, the *Whydah* boasted a complement of about 150 men, all crammed into a ship that measured thirty feet wide and one hundred feet long. With the bulk of the pirates' booty stored on the *Whydah*, the decks were probably starting to sag. Along with such items as "elephant tusks, sugar, molasses, rum, cloth… indigo, and… dry goods…there was the precious metal, 180 sacks of coins, each… weighing fifty pounds."[48] What this meant was the *Whydah* would have been very low in the water, a dangerous condition in a storm.

Throughout the afternoon a dense fog had rolled in, what should have been an early storm warning for the pirates. In the late afternoon the storm itself began. Instead of steering out to sea, Bellamy chose to stay close to the land, a move which leads many to believe he did indeed wish to try and make port somewhere in Cape Cod.

Sometime after 5pm Samuel Bellamy ordered all three ships to light lanterns on their sterns, a common navigational aid. But conditions continued to get worse.

"An arctic storm from Canada was driving into the warm air that had swept up the coast from the Caribbean. The last gasp of a frigid New England winter, the cold front was about to combine with the warm front in one of the worst storms everr to hit the Cape."[49] "According to eyewitness accounts, gusts topped 70 miles [113 kilometers] an hour and the seas rose to 30 feet. [9 meters]."[50]

Graphic courtesy Shodor.org.

Square-rigged ships like the *Whydah Galley* did not handle so well in high winds, and since the winds were coming from the northeast, it was now pretty much out of the question for Bellamy to even try to attempt to head back out to sea. With each swell, the ship would have been pushed west by the winds, no matter how hard the pirates tried to keep heading north. One or more of them would have heard the crash of waves hitting the shore and shouted, "Breakers, breakers!" But it was simply too late.

The accident was succinctly described by Thomas Davis in his deposition before his trial for piracy in Boston, Massachusetts, in October of 1717:

The Ship being at an Anchor, they cut their Cables and ran a shoar, in a quarter of an hour after the Ship struck, the Main-mast was carried by the board, and in the Morning She was beat to pieces. About Sixteen Prisoners drown'd, Crumpstey Master of the Pink being one, and One hundred and forty-four in all.[51]

"Although the beach was just 500 feet away, the bitter ocean temperatures were cold enough to kill the strongest swimmer within minutes. Other crew members were crushed by the weight of falling rigging, cannon, and cargo as the ship, her treasure, and the remaining men on board plunged to the ocean floor, swallowed up by the shifting sands of the cape."[52] Anyone reaching the shore would then be faced with the challenge of climbing the seventy-foot cliffs (now called Marconi Beach).

When local residents arrived on the beach the next morning, "more than a hundred mutilated corpses lay at the wrack line with the ship's timbers."[53] Since the locals had no way of knowing how many men were on board the ship and obviously no knowledge of their names, individual corpses were not identified.

Around noon that same day nine men were arrested in suspicion of piracy. They had washed ashore off Wellfleet and were taken into the home of a local resident, where one of the original crew members of the Mary Anne, Alexander Mackonacky, exposed them as members of Bellamy's crew.

First taken to Barnstable Gaol in Wellfleet and then to Boston Gaol the next day by horseback, Hendrick Quintor, Thomas South, Peter Cornelius Hoof, John Shuan, Thomas Baker, John Brown, Simon Van Vorst and Thomas Davis were tried in Boston, Massachusetts on 18 October 1717. South was the only one the court believed was a forced man and was acquitted. John Julian, also arrested that day, was sold into slavery. Davis was tried separately and also found not guilty.

Cape Cod folklore has many stories about a man who began to be seen not long after the wreck. The most famous reference to him is made by Henry David Thoreau, who wrote about the wreck of the *Whydah* and this stranger:

In the year 1717, a noted pirate named Bellamy was led on to the bar at Wellfleet by the captain of a snow which he had taken, to whom he had offered his vessel again if he would pilot him into Provincetown Harbor. Tradition says that the latter threw over a burning tar-barrel in the night, which drifted ashore; and the pirates followed it. A storm coming on, their whole fleet was wrecked, and more than hundred dead bodies lay along the shore. Six who escaped shipwreck were executed.

"At times to this day," (1793) says the historian of Wellfleet, "there are King William and Queen Mary's coppers picked up, and pieces of silver called cob-money. The violence of the seas moves the sands on the outer bar, so that at times the iron caboose of the ship [that is, Bellamy's] at low ebbs has been seen."

Another tells us that, "For many years after this shipwreck, a man of a very singular and frightful aspect used every spring and autumn to be seen traveling on the Cape, who was supposed to have been one of Bellamy's crew. The presumption is that he went to some place where money had been secreted by the pirates, to get such a supply as his exigencies required. When he died, many pieces of gold were found in a girdle which he constantly wore."[54]

Before the days of filing birth certificates with the county clerk and the Internet, it was not difficult for someone who wanted to escape the authorities to head a few towns away in any direction, make up a name, and start a new life.

The tales say that at night passersby could hear screams and wails of torment and shouts of entreaty from within this man's cabin. It as imagined that he was haunted by demons or the ghosts of his past crimes he had committed while pursuing a life of piracy.

Older tales told about how he frequently spent evenings in private houses, taking advantage of their hospitality to get free meals. If they had trouble getting him to leave, they simply started reading from the Bible or holding family devotions, causing him to leave.

Then, suddenly, they stopped seeing him. Some presumed he had traveled into Boston or another port and found work on a ship. Finally, someone was brave enough to enter his cabin, where he was found dead. Around his waist was a girdle filled with gold coins. He had claw marks around his neck.

Among the many tales of this stranger is this one, which happened many years after the wreck:

One October [evening] in the year 1782, a resident of Eastham, after a great storm, decided to hike down along the beach toward the lower Cape, and reached the scene where the Whidaw *had been wrecked... Far in the distance he saw a bonfire, and hastened toward it. Upon drawing closer, he discovered the same mysterious character known to almost every resident of that section.*

This sinister individual, with a cocked pistol at his side, was three feet down, in a hole in the sand, and had just struck the top of a chest. The Eastham resident, in his excitement, dislodged a bit of material from the top of the cliff where he was walking, and the pirate, with an oath, sprang for his pistol.

The Cape Cod resident ran for the underbrush and escaped, but not before a close call from one of the pirate's bullets. He returned several days later by daytime, but never found anything. The pirate was later found dead by the roadside with gold doubloons in his money belt.[55]

This last story in quite improbable, but the idea that someone could have survived the wreck is not impossible. Record-keeping in the early 1700s was rudimentary at best. And nearly all folklore has its basis in reality.

"The Unknown Survivor" originally published in June of 2014 in the online newsletter *Pirates and Privateers* on the website *Thistles and Pirates.*

Sam Bellamy & Olivier Levasseur – Two Pirates Just Kickin' Around the Caribbean

For a few months in 1716 Samuel Bellamy and Olivier Levasseur were the terror of the Caribbean, capturing an estimated fifty ships during their travels. While most pirate crews traveled aimlessly, voting on destinations as they went, Bellamy and Levasseur seemed to head in a definite direction: toward the area of Cape Cod, Massachusetts. Some sources say they headed that way because Bellamy was eager to reunite with a sweetheart; others say their intention was to establish their own pirate republic in Maine.

There are two versions of when Olivier Levasseur first appeared in the historical records. Former captive Jeremiah Higgins stated that he didn't appear until after Bellamy had a falling out with Benjamin Hornigold over whether to attack English ships. Bellamy had been in command of the sloop *Mary Anne* and sailed in consort with Hornigold when this fallout happened.

Higgins's tale, given in his deposition before his trial for piracy in New York in 1717, described how he was forced to join the pirates; how Hornigold was voted out of the company; and how they met up with Levasseur.

That about Two & Twenty months ago he sailed out of Jamaica a foremastman on Board a certain Sloop called the Blackett, *Abraham Lamb Master, bound for the wrecks on the coast of Florida. That before they came to the wrecks, one Capt. Hornigold Commander of a Pyrate Sloop called the* Benjamin *came on board their sloop and after some time Desired the Examinate and some other of the Men belonging to the said Sloop* Blackett *to row him on board the said sloop* Benjamin *which they did and after they were aboard the said Sloop [He] refused to let the Examinant and one John Fletcher his companion Returne to their Sloop* Blackett *againe but detained them and Altho their Master Abraham Lamb came on Board and prayed the said Hornigold to Release his said Men Yet he utterly refused to do so but detained them and Carryed them away by force against their Wills.*

That the said Sloop Benjamin *afterwards sailed to the coast of the Havana having upwards of Eighty Men on Board, and off the Coast of the Havana at a place called Porta Maria they took the Sloop* Mary Anne *then belonging to the French & Spaniards Loaded with Dry Goods and Liquors, and then the Pyrates Divided their company and putt some of the company on Board the* Mary Anne *and chose on Samuel Bellamy to be Commander of both sloops and Turned out Hornigold and for some time after consorted together with the said Sloops until a quarrel happened among the Company and then they gave the said Sloop* Benjamin *to the said Hornigold and some Company and parted from him detaining the Examinate on board the said Sloop* Mary Anne.

That afterwards the said Sloop Mary Anne *Cruizing about from place to place met with another Pyrate sloop called the* Postillion *off Cape Mayos, one Capt. La Boos Commander with whom they consorted and cruised about...*[56]

Another version of the story has Olivier Levasseur already sailing with Hornigold before the falling out over the attacking of English ships happened.

In his interrogation before his trial for piracy in Boston, Massachusetts, on Monday, 6 May 1717, John Brown, who became a member of Samuel Bellamy's crew and would ultimately be hanged for piracy in November, told of his time as Olivier Levasseur's captive and how Bellamy and Hornigold quarreled and went their separate ways.

About a year ago he belonged to a Ship Commanded by Capt. Kingston, which In her Voyage with Logwood to Holland was taken to the Leeward of the Havanas by two piratical Sloops, one Commanded by Hornygold and the other By a Frenchman called Labous, each having 70 Men on Board. The Pirates kept the Ship about 8 or 10 Days and then having taken out of her what they thought proper delivered her back to some of the Men, who belonged to her. Labous kept the Examinate on board his Sloop about 4 months, the English Sloop under Hornygold's command keeping company with them all that time...

From thence they Sailed on to Hispaniola in the latter end of May, where they tarryed about 3 Months. The Examinate then left Labous and went on board the Sloop Commanded formerly by Hornygold, at that time by one Bellamy, who upon a difference arising amongst the English Pirates because Hornygold refused to take and plunder English Vessels, was chosen by a great Majority their Captain & Hornygold departed with 26 hand in a prize Sloop, Bellamy having then on Board about 50 men, most of them English.[57]

What is known is that after they parted company with Hornigold, Bellamy and Levasseur sailed eastward in consort.[58]

Olivier Levasseur was known by many names: Olivier or Oliver La Buse, Louis Labous, and Oliver de la Bouche, just to name a few. His nicknames were *La Buse* (French for "the Buzzard," – earned because of the speed and ruthlessness with which he attacked his targets) and *la Bouche* (French for "the Mouth"). Adding to the confusion, Levasseur apparently had the habit of altering his name at will, causing people who encountered him to come away with a different name each time.[59]

The only information historians agree on regarding Levasseur is that he was born (or was a native of) Calais, France, to a bourgeois family and received an excellent education.[60] Historians give his birth date as sometime during the time of the Nine Years' War (1688-1697).

However he got his start, by 1716 he was sailing around the Caribbean with Samuel Bellamy, attacking and plundering ships and collecting treasure as they went. Between attacks they sometimes found remote islands where their ships could be cleaned and readied for their next attack.

Bellamy and Levasuer's story is one of many conquests. During their travels around the Caribbean they went such places as Cape Corante, the Isle of Pines, and Hispaniola.

During September 1716 off the coast of Puerto Rico, the pirates attempted to attack a 44-gun French ship. "After an hour-long fight, [they were] driven off with little loss."[61] October found them plundering ships along the north coast of Hispaniola. In November and December, Bellamy and Levasseur took up residence on the island of St. Croix for a few weeks, using it as a base to take "at least a dozen ships in the Virgin and Leeward Island."[62]

Part of the reason for their ease in capturing vessels was the reputation established by previous pirates who had tortured sailors, particularly captains, who did not immediately surrender upon being approached by a ship bearing a Jolly Roger and firing a shot across their bow. The early 1700s was a time of low (and sometimes no) pay for sailors, with generally no chance of advancement. Most did not feel any loyalty toward their captain or the company that owned whatever ship they served on, and thus saw no reason to sacrifice themselves defending the ship. Most hoped that by giving up and staying out of the way they would survive the pirate encounter unscathed. That being said, "There is no record that Captain Bellamy and his crew ever used force or violence to capture any of the scores of vessels they plundered."[63]

An interesting incident occurred while Bellamy & Levasseur sailed together. When they captured a ship named the *Bonetta*, Bellamy allowed a boy named John King to join his pirate crew. In the early 1700s it was not unusual for a boy from a poor family to sign aboard a ship as a cabin boy or powder monkey. It was an opportunity to learn a trade and earn a living. But John King came from a family of means. When he joined the pirates, he wore French woven-silk stockings and leather shoes fastened with buckles, both reflecting "18th-century upper-class style."[64]

In his deposition about the capture of the *Bonetta*, her master Abijah Savage said that on 9 November two large sloops chased him for about six and one-half hours. He gave the names of the pirate captains, some information about Levasseur's crew, and told the tale of John King, who willingly joined the pirates.

One of the said Sloops called the Mary Anne *was Commanded as he was told by one Samuel Bellamy, who declared himself to be an Englishman born in London, and that the other, called the* Postillion *was Commanded by one Louis de Boure who was a French Man, and has his Sloop chiefly Navigated with men of that Nation. That each of the said Sloops was mounted with Eight Guns and had betwixt Eighty or Ninety Men apiece on Board...*

[H]e could not learn the Names of any of the Men on board the Postillion *excepting the Quarter Master, who went by the name of De Lorme...*

[O]ne John King who was coming as a Passenger with him from the Said Island of Jamaica to the Island of Antigua deserted his Sloop, and went with the Pirates, and was so far from being forced or compelled by them as the Deponent could perceive or learn, that he declared he would kill himself if he was restrained, and even threatened his Mother who was then on board as a passenger with the Deponent.[65]

Researchers estimate that John King could have been as young as eight years old when he joined the pirates. Excavations of the wreck of the *Whydah*, Bellamy's ship, found the fibula of a young boy along with a silk stocking and one leather shoe.[66]

When Bellamy and Levasseur caught up with Savage's ship, they fired their guns and hoisted their black flags, at which point the *Bonetta's* master struck his sails and lowered his boat to go meet with them. The pirates detained him, his crew, and the passengers until 24 November. Before letting them go, they took some of their clothes, other items, a black man, and an Indian boy.

After they were finished with the *Bonetta* in late November 1716, the pirates sailed towards the Caribbean island of Saba, a five-square mile islet located off the Virgin Islands. There they chased and captured two ships, one of which was the *Sultana* commanded by Captain Richards. According to pirate John Brown, "Having plundered the Ships and taken out some Young Men they dismist the rest… and made a Man of War of Richard's [vessel], which they put under the Command of Bellamy, and appointed Paulsgrave Williams Captain of the Sloop."[67]

Near the island of Blanco, sometime around January 1717, Bellamy and Levasseur parted company. Some sources say they were separated by a storm, and others that Levasseur's crew simply voted to strike out on their own in another direction. Whatever the exact reason for the separation, their parting was propitious: Bellamy and the majority of his band of pirates perished in a storm off Cape Cod, Massachusetts, on 26 April 1717.

Historians differ as to where exactly Levasseur went between his parting from Bellamy and his arrival in Nassau in the Bahamas.[68] One recorded sighting occurred off the coast of New England on 4 July 1717, when he was in command of a 250-ton ship with twenty guns and two hundred men from various nations. One crewman, Mr. Main, was reportedly the chief negotiator with their captives.

On this date, "La Buse's gang plundered a sloop from Portsmouth, New Hampshire, off the coast of Virginia; the pirates told the ship's captain, John Frost, that they were headed for the New England coast where they "had a consort ship of twenty guns."[69]

Captain Frost later said the pirates chased him for twelve hours, finally catching up to him at nine o'clock in the evening. In David Cordingly's book *Under the Black Flag*, Levasseur's ship had twenty guns and a crew of 170.

She fired a broadside of 'double round and partridges, and a volley of small shot,' which meant that each of the ten guns on one side of the ship was loaded with two round cannonballs and a bag of partridge shot. This would have been a lethal combination at close range, and it was accompanied by a volley of fire from the muskets and pistols. The bombardment beat the men off the deck and so shattered the hull, rigging, and sails of Frost's ship that he surrendered without a fight.[70]

Frost was ordered to board but sent his Mate instead. The Mate was met with words and told that if he had been the Master, they would have cut him down for trying to run from them. When Frost finally did go on board the pirate ship in the morning, he was used roughly until Mr. Main attempted to "make things easy" between the pirates and Frost.[71]

Then Levasseur's quartermaster and some other pirates boarded Frost's ship and helped themselves to "40 Hogsheads of Rhum, one Hogshead and several Barrels of Sugar, some Money, Watches, a Negro Man, one of the Pumps," and some linens, woolens, bedding, and various other items.[72]

A couple of other ships happened along while Frost's ship was being plundered, and the pirates promptly plundered them also. When they were done, Levasseur sent Frost back aboard the merchant ship, at which point Levasseur's quartermaster and other crew members stripped Frost down to his shirt, cut and beat him, and threatened to skin and barbecue him. Belatedly becoming aware of the fracas, Levasseur fired a shot and ordered his crew back aboard the pirate ship.

Eight days later, Levasuer took a ship named the *Dispatch* in the vicinity of the Damariscove, Monhegan, and Matinicus islands of Maine. The ship's master, Joseph Christophers, described his attacker as a "Ship of 250 Tons,

20 Guns, about 200 men, who ordered him in French and then in English to strike unto a Pirate, hoist out his Boat and come on board.[73] When the pirates learned that he had neglected to bring his ship's papers with him, "They beat Christophers with about 40 stripes on his back and sent for his Papers." [74]

They then took a "Hogshead of Bear, a Hogshead of Water, half of his Bread," and assorted other items, such as brandy, wine, and clothes.[75] Most of the master's papers and letters were thrown overboard. The *BostonNewsletter* identified the pirates as being the same ones who, only a few days earlier, had robbed Captain Frost, This was the last reported incident of piracy in New England for many months.[76]

There is some speculation that Olivier Levasseur was in this vicinity to pursue the building of a pirate stronghold or to recover booty already buried in Machias, Maine. Local folklore tells of a cache of gold, silver, and jewels left by pirates a few miles northwest of Machias. According to the April 2015 issue of *Lost Treasure Magazine*, there used to be visible evidence of earthworks and rotten logs "up until the 1970's", but no one has ever actually found physical evidence of such a cache.

Sometime between September and December 1717, Levasseur arrived in Nassau. During these four months, Paulsgrave Williams – Bellamy's friend and cohort who missed perishing in the storm that killed Bellamy because he had temporarily separated from him and gone to Block Island – reentered Levasseur's life when he sailed into Nassau harbor in the same *Mary Anne* that Bellamy originally commanded.

The *Mary Anne* was now in pitiful condition. During the journey from New England to Nassau most of her crewmen had died of starvation or deserted. She was followed by the *Anne Galley* commanded by Richard Noland, also a former crewmember of Bellamy's. Together they announced the demise of Bellamy.[77]

Some references from 1717 have Levasseur flying a white ensign, rather than a black one, for his pirate flag. One such sighting happened while Governor Walter Hamilton of the Leeward Islands was touring the Virgin

Islands in a ship called the *Seaford*. They had just turned around to begin their return journey to Antigua when they encountered a "pirate ship 'of about 26 guns and 250 men.' Off St. Thomas. The ship flew a 'white ensign with a figure of a dead man spread in it' and, according to Captain Rose, was commanded by none other than Olivier La Buse."[78] Despite being out-gunned, Captain Rose tried to chase the pirates, but was out-sailed by Levasseur.

A possible reference to Levasseur between the time he left New England and reached Nassau comes from a note "on the flyleaf of a well-worn edition of Jeremy Taylor's *Holy Living and Holy Dying*. The handwritten inscription reads: 'Septr. 28th: 1717 at 8 in the morning in ye Lat. Of 32 degrees 8 minutes about 160 Leag: west from Madeira we were attacked by a French Pirate with Death's head in black in ye middle of a white ensign, and by the Providence of God were delivered, altho' they were once so neare that there shott flew a great way over us, and were Likewise once a head of uss.' "[79]

The last recorded encounter with Levasseur in the Caribbean happened on 12 June 1718. Captain Frances Hume, commanding HMS *Scarborough*, nearly captured Levasseur while his ship was anchored at La Blanquilla and he was preoccupied with plundering a small prize sloop, Levasseur and the majority of his crew managed to escape in their faster vessel.

From the Caribbean it has been generally assumed that Levasseur sailed for the Indian Ocean, thus avoiding the arrival of Woodes Rogers there in Nassau in July 1718. It is not entirely impossible that he returned to Maine to build a stronghold or dig up a hidden cache of treasure. Eventually Levasseur would be captured on Reunion Island and hanged for piracy on 7 July 1730.

"Samuel Bellamy and Olivier Levasseur – Two Pirates Just Kickin' Around the Caribbean" originally published in July and August of 2015 in the online newsletter *Pirates and Privateers* on the website *Thistles and Pirates*.

John King – The Boy Pirate

In the Caribbean in 1716, Samuel Bellamy terrorized shipping by robbing vessels and passengers of their cargo and valuables. During his course of depredations, he captured the *Bonetta*. Over the fifteen days that he plundered the ship, he allowed a boy named John King to join his crew.

In the early 1700s it was not that unusual for boys from poor families to sign aboard a ship as cabin boys (a type of servant to an officer) or powder monkey.[80] It was an opportunity to learn a trade from which to earn a living. Boys were sometimes no older than eight when they signed aboard a ship. Going to sea probably looked better to some than being a chimney sweep or becoming a child laborer. It only took a few years for a boy to learn enough to assume the duties of an adult sailor.

But King was different. His family had money. At the time he joined the pirates he wore French woven-silk stockings and leather shoes fastened with buckles, both of which reflected "18th-century upper-class style".[81]

In Master Abijah Savage's deposition about the capture of his ship – given before Walter Hamilton, Esq., Captain General and Governor in Chief of all His Majesty's Leeward Caribbean Islands – he said that on the 9th of November while traveling from Jamaica to Antigua, he met with two large sloops which chased him for about six and a half hours.

When the ships caught up with him, they fired a cannon and hoisted a black flag at the mast, at which point he struck his sails and lowered his boat to go meet with them. Samuel Bellamy detained his crew and passengers until 24 November. Before letting them go, however, the pirates took some of their clothes, various items, a black man, and an Indian boy.

In his deposition, Savage gave a description of the two ships:

One of the said Sloops called the Mary Anne *was Commanded as he was told by one Samuel Bellamy who declared himself to be an Englishman born in London, and that the other, called the* Postillion *was Commanded by one Louis de Boure who was a French Man, and has his Sloop chiefly Navigated with men of that Nation. That each of the said Sloops was mounted with Eight Guns and had betwixt Eighty or Ninety Men apiece in Board....*[82]

Savage then goes on to tell the story of "one John King who was coming as a Passenger with him from the Said Island of Jamaica to the Island of Antigua deserted his Sloop, and went with the Pirates, and was so far from being forced or compelled by them as the Deponent could perceive or learn, that he declared he would kill himself if he was restrained, and even threatened his Mother who was then on board as a passenger with the Deponent."[83]

Ongoing excavations of the wreck of Bellamy's *Whydah Galley* found a leg bone, or fibula, along with a silk stocking and a leather shoe (right).[84] When these items were first discovered, most thought they belonged to a small man. But Barry Clifford, head of the expedition, "showed the short fibula to expedition archaeologist John de Bry, and Smithsonian Institution expert David Hunt. Both agreed that the fibula belonged to a child age 8 to 11."[85]

Kenneth J Kinkor, *Whydah* researcher and maritime historian, said, "The stocking is made of woven French silk, and the shoe – which is only 2 inches in width at its widest point – is of upper-class design and craftsmanship, consistent with it belonging to John King."[86]

There were many reasons that the life of a pirate might have appealed to a young boy like King. Kinkor speculated he might have been attracted to "a free and easy lifestyle, and a classless democratic subculture.[87]

Since his clothing indicated that he likely came from a more well-to-do family, perhaps the chance to break away from the class restrictions and expectations of his day were what attracted him. If you asked my friends who raised boys, it would be the chance to get away from being ordered around by his parents, carrying a sword, bossing people around and seeing them be afraid of him, and not having to bathe.

King's new life as a pirate likely included many adventures, but also some new responsibilities. Not long after he joined them, the pirates anchored at St. Croix, where they spent a couple of months enjoying the spoils of their conquests. During their stay, three men tried to run away. One was captured and brought back. As punishment he was severely whipped with a cat-o'nine-tails. [88]

All new pirates had to sign the ship's articles before they were accepted as full members of the crew. Each crew devised their own set of rules, but they shared some similarities. For example, Bartholomew Roberts's list included:

Every man to have Equal Right to ye Provisions or Liquors at any time & use them at Pleasure, unless Scarcity makes a Restriction necessary for ye Good of all.

Any man who should Defraud ye Company, or another, to ye Vallew of a Dollar, he shall suffer Punishment as ye Company deeme ffit.

Any man who Deserts ye Company, keeps any Secret, or Deserts his Station in Time of Battle, shall be punished by Death, Marooning, or Whipping, as ye Company shall deeme ffit & Just.[89]

In addition, each member of the crew was entitled to an equal share of whatever profit was made during the voyage.

Every member of the crew had assigned duties to perform, determined by a watch bill, or duty roster. Unfortunately, it's unknown what duties a boy like King would have been given.

Early in 1717 Bellamy and his crew spotted the *Whydah Galley* sailing past the Bahamas and gave chase. She was completing a voyage of what was known as the "middle passage," a term used for ships sailing between the African coast and the Caribbean slave markets. This was a lucrative trade in the early 1700s. After selling her slaves in the Caribbean, she had been loaded with coins and other trade goods intended for sale in England.

After being chased for three days the captain of the *Whydah*, Lawrence Prince, surrendered without a fight. This was normal behavior during this period; Prince hoped that if he surrendered without resisting his crew might avoid being beaten or tortured, as was known to happen at the hands of pirates. Since Captain Prince gave in so quickly, Bellamy allowed him and the members of his crew who desired to leave to sail away in Bellamy's old ship the *Sultana*. The pirates claimed the *Whydah* as their own.

26 April 1717 started out like any other day for the pirates. In the morning, they captured "a pink with more than 7,000 gallons of Madeira wine on board" and "a small sloop with a cargo of deer hides and tobacco, in the afternoon."[90] Per customary pirate procedure, smaller groups were sent over to the ships from the *Whydah* to act as the new crews of their prizes.

Bellamy and his crew were sailing north along the east coast of the American Colonies. Cape Cod folklore says their destination was Eastham, Massachusetts, where Bellamy intended to pick up Maria Hallett, believed to be his lover on their way to Rhode Island or Maine. He might also have been hoping to sell some of their booty.

At this time, the *Whydah* boasted a crew of approximately 150 men, all crammed into a ship that measured about thirty feet wide and one hundred feet long. With the bulk of the pirate's booty stored on the *Whydah*, the decks were probably starting to sag. Along with such items as "[e]lephant tusks, sugar, molasses, rum, cloth, quinine bark, indigo, and… dry goods," there were 180 sacks of coins, weighing fifty pounds each.[91]

What this meant was that the *Whydah* would have been very low in the water, a dangerous condition for a ship in a storm.[92]

That evening a dense fog rolled in, which should have been an early warning for the pirates, and the storm began to manifest itself. The capture of the *Fisher* that afternoon helped the pirates to navigate through the increasing fog. Instead of steering out to sea, Bellamy chose to stay close to land, a move which leads many to believe that he did indeed wish to try and make port somewhere in Cape Cod.

Sometime after 5:00pm, Samuel Bellamy ordered all three ships to light lanterns on their sterns, a common navigational aide. Conditions continued to worsen. "An Arctic storm from Canada was driving into the warm air that had swept up the coast from the Caribbean. The last gasp of a frigid New England winter, the cold front was about to combine with the warm front in one of the worst storms ever to hit the Cape."[93]

"According to eyewitness accounts, gusts topped 70 miles [113 kilometers] an hour and the seas rose to 30 feet [9 meters]."[94]

Square-rigged ships like the *Whydah Galley* did not handle so well in high winds, and since the winds were coming from the northeast, it was now pretty much out of the question for Bellamy to even attempt to try to head back out to sea. With each swell, the ship was pushed west by the winds, no matter how hard the pirates tried to keep heading north. Then one of them would have heard the crash of the waves hitting the shore and shouted "Breakers, breakers!" But it was simply too late. The accident was succinctly described by Thomas Davis in his deposition before his trial for piracy in Boston, Massachusetts, in October of 1717:

Ship being at an Anchor, they cut their Cables and ran a shoar, in a quarter of an hour after the Ship struck, the Main-mast was carried by the board, and in the Morning She was beat to pieces. About Sixteen Prisoners drown'd, Crumpstey Master of the Pink being one, and One hundred and forty-four in all.[95]

What Davis is saying here was that the pirates attempted to save themselves by anchoring the ship to the sea bottom. When the anchors dragged, meaning they failed to get a grip on the sea bed, they cut the cables. They then made a last-ditch effort to save themselves by trying to turn the ship into the wind. But the *Whydah* was so heavy she slid back down a wave and crashed into a sand bar, spelling the end of the ship and all but two members of her crew.

Although the beach was just 500 feet away, the bitter ocean temperatures were cold enough to kill the strongest swimmer within minutes. Other crew members were crushed by the weight of falling rigging, cannons, and cargo as the ship, her treasure, and the remaining men on board plunged to the ocean floor, swallowed up by the shifting sands of the cape.[96]

Locals arrived on the shore the next morning to find "more than a hundred mutilated corpses lay at the wrack line with the ship's timbers."[97] But King's body was not among them. During excavation of the wreck site it was determined that he died because one of the cannons had pinned him to the seabed.

John King is the youngest recorded member of a pirate crew during the Golden Age of Piracy. His time as a pirate lasted for three months.

"John King – The Boy Pirate" originally published in November of 2015 in the online newsletter *Pirates and Privateers* on the website *Thistles and Pirates*.

The Trials of Eight Persons Indited for Piracy

A reprint of the trials for piracy of the men from the *Whydah Galley*.
THE TRIALS Of Eight Persons Indited for Piracy &c.
Of whom Two were acquitted, and the rest found Guilty.

At a Justiciary Court of Admiralty Assembled and Held in Boston within His Majesty's Province of the Massachusetts-Bay in New-England, on the 18th of October 1717. and by several Adjournments continued to the 30th. Pursuant to His Majesty's Commission and Instructions, founded on the Act of Parliament Made in the 11th. & 12th of KING William IIId. Intituled, An Act for the more effectual Suppression of Piracy.

With an APPENDIX, Containing the Substance of their Confessions given before His Excellency the Governour, when they were first brought to Boston, and committed to Goal.

Boston: Printed by B. Green, for John Edwards, and Sold at his Shop in King's Street. 1718.

I Do appoint Bartholomew Green to Print the Trials of Simon Van Vorst, John Brown, Thomas Baker, Hendrick Quintor, Peter Cornelius Hoof, John Shuan, Thomas South, and Thomas Davis, To be Sold by John Edwards, Bookseller in King Street, Boston; And that no other Person presume to Print the same.

SAMUEL SHUTE.

Boston, May 22d. 1718.

Anno Regni Regis GEORGII, Quarto,

At a Justiciary Court of Admiralty held in the Court House in Boston, for and within His Majesty's Province of the Massachusetts-Bay in New-England on Friday the Eighteen Day of October, Anno Domini, 1717. by His Majesty's Commissioners especially Appointed and Cited, as the Law Directs, to Try, Hear and Adjudge Cases of Piracy, Robbery and Felony Committed on the High Seas, viz.

His Excellency Samuel Shute Esq Captain General, Governour, and Commander in Chief of this Province, and Vice Admiral, &c. President. The Honourable William Dummer Esq Lieutenant Governour of the Province. The Honourable Andrew Belcher, John Cushing, Nathaniel Norden, John Wheelwright, Benjamin Lynde, Thomas Hutchinson, and Thomas Pitch, Esqrs of His Majesty's Council for this Province. John Meinzies Esq Judge of the Vice Admiralty. Capt. Thomas Smart Commander of His Majesty's Ship of War the Squirrel, John Jekyll Esq Collector of the Plantation Duties.

HIS Excellency the Governour with the Commissioners above-named being Assembled, Upon the Motion of His Majesty's Advocate, The Statute Made in the Eleventh and Twelfth Years of King William the Third, with the several Continuations of it; Her late Majesty Queen Ann's Royal Commission of the 20th of October, in the Third Year of Her Reign, Pursuant to the abovesaid Act, under the Broad Seal of England, Constituting the Court, &c. The Proclamation Declaring His Present Majesty's Pleasure for continuing the Officers of His Majesty's Plantations till His Majesty's Pleasure should be further Declared, And also his Excellency's Commission & Instructions from the Crown were openly Read; and the Court Solemnly & Publickly called and proclaimed, and then his Excellency the Governour in the first Place took the Oath appointed in the said Act, And immediately after Administered the same Oath to the several Commissioners.

And then Samuel Tyley Gent Notary Publick was Sworn Register of the Court by the President. The Statute Directing that the Register of this Court shall be a Publick Notary. But the Judge of Admiralty and Advocate G. insisted, That the Register of the Court of Admiralty was the only Person lawfully qualified to act as Register on this occasion, he being by vertue of his Office a Notary Publick in matters within Admiralty Jurisdiction.

And immediately after the Court Issued out a Warrant signed by the Register, Directed to the Sheriffs of the County of Suffolk in the Province aforesaid, requiring them forthwith to bring into Court the Bodies of Simon Van Vorst, John Brown, Thomas South, Thomas Baker, Hendrick Quintor, Peter Cornelius Hoof, and John Shuan, from His Majesty's Goal in Boston, they being Accused of and Imprisoned for Piracy, Robbery and Felony committed on the high Sea.

And accordingly the Sheriffs brought the Prisoners into Court, and having hold up their hands at the Bar, the Indictment Exhibited against them by Mr. Smith His Majesty's Advocate was Read to them by the Register, and is as follows:

Cur. Justic. Admir. Boston. Amer. Hab. Indictment of Simon Van Vorst, John Brown, Thomas South, Thomas Baker, Hendrick Quintor, Peter Cornelius Hoof, and John Shuan, for Crimes of Piracy, Robbery & Felony committed on the high Sea.

ALbeit the Crimes of Piracy and Robbery are most Odious and Detestable, being Repugnant to the Laws of Almighty God, Destructive of Government, and Directly Tending to Subvert and Extinguish the Natural and Civil Rights of Mankind, and therefore are strictly Prohibited and Provided against by divers Express Laws, Statutes and Ordinances of our Sovereign Lord the King, and more particularly by an Act of Parliament, Made in the Eleventh and Twelfth Years of the Reign of King William the Third, Entituled, An Act for the more Effectual Suppression of Piracy; Whereby it is Enacted and Ordained,

That such Persons, as shall be attainted & found Guilty of Piracy, Robbery & Felony committed in, or upon the Sea, or in any Haven, River, Creek or Place where the Admiral or Admirals have Power, Authority or Jurisdiction, by their own Confessions, or their Refusing to Plead, or upon the Oath of Witnesses by Process founded on the Authority of His Majesty's Commission or Commissions by the said Act directed and appointed, shall be Executed and put to Death, and also to suffer Loss of Lands, Goods and Chattles; as in and by the said Act, which was Revived and Confirmed in the first Year of our Sovereign Lord the King, and still continues and remains in full force, will more clearly appear.

Nevertheless so it is, That the said Simon Van Vorst, John Brown, Thomas South, Thomas Baker, Hendrick Quintor, Peter Cornelius Hoof, and John Shuan, To the high displeasure of Almighty God, in open Violation of the Rights of Nations and Mankind, and in Contempt and Defyance of His Majesty's good and wholesome Laws aforesaid, Wilfully, Wickedly, and Feloniously, all and each of them, being Principal Actors and Contrivers, Associates, Confederates, and Accomplices, Did, Perpetrated and Committed on the high Sea sundry Facts of Piracy and Robbery, Distinctly Specified and Expressed, and Qualified with respect to time and place, and manner, when, and where, and in which the said Facts were so done, perpetrated and committed by all and each of them, the said Simon Van Vorst, John Brown, Thomas South, Thomas Baker, Hendrick Quintor, Peter Cornelius Hoof, and John Shuan, in the several Articles immediately following, Viz.

I. And first, the said Simon Van Vorst, John Brown, Thomas South, Thomas Baker, Hendrick Quintor, Peter Cornelius Hoof, & John Shuan, on or about the Twentieth & Sixth day of April last past without lawful Cause or Warrant, in Hostile manner with Force & Arms, Piratically & Felonionsly did surprize, Assault, Invade, and Enter on the High Sea, viz. Between St. Georges Banks and Nantucket Shoalls, a free Trading Vessel or Pink, called the Mary Anne of Dublin, bound from this Harbour to His Majesty's Colony of New-York, which said Vessel or Pink was owned by His Majesty's Subjects of Ireland, having on board her own Cargoe, and Navigated by her own Crew, belonging to His Majesty's Kingdom aforesaid.

II. Secondly, The said Simon Van Vorst, John Brown, Thomas South, Thomas Baker, Hendrick Quintor, Peter Cornelius Hoof, and John Shuan, having in manner aforesaid, entered the said Vessel or Pink, did at the same time and place, aforesaid, Piratically and Feloniously seize and imprison Andrew Crumpstey Master thereof, and him the said Crumpstey did force & constrain with five of his Crew to leave and abandon the said Vessel or Pink, and to go on board a Ship named the Whido, which Ship was then imployed and exercised by the said Simon Van Vorst, John Brown, Thomas South, Thomas Baker, Hendrick Quintor, Peter Cornelius Hoof, and John

Shuan, and others their Accomplices and Confederates in continued acts of Piracy & Robbery on this, and other Coasts of America.

III. Thirdly, The said Simon Van Vorst, John Brown, Thomas South, Thomas Baker, Hendrick Quintor, Peter Cornelius Hoof, & John Shuan, Did on the day, and at the place aforesaid, Piratically and Feloniously Imbezil, Spoil and Rob the Cargoe, of the said Vessel or Pink, consisting chiefly of Wines, and also the Goods & Wearing Apparel of the said Master and his Crew.

IV. Fourthly, The said Simon Van Vorst, John Brown, Thomas South, Thomas Baker, Hendrick Quintor, Peter Cornelius Hoof, and John Shuan, having at the time and place, and in manner aforesaid, over powered and subdued the said Master and his Crew, and made themselves Masters of the said Vessel or Pink, did then and there Piratically and Feloniously Steer and Direct their Course after the above-named Piratical Ship, the Whido, intending to joyn and accompany the same; and thereby, to enable themselves better to pursue and accomplish their Execrable designs to oppress the Innocent, and cover the Sea with Depredations and Robberies.

All which Facts of Piracy, Robbery and Felony having been done, perpetrated and committed at the time and place, and in manner aforesaid, by the said Simon Van Vorst, John Brown, Thomas South, Thomas Baker, Hendrick Quintor, Peter Cornelius Hoof, and John Shuan, all and each of them being principal Actors and Contrivers, Associates, Accomplices and Confederates in the said Crimes, and being thereof Convicted and Attainted upon sufficient Proof, made by clear and plenary Evidence before His Majesty's Commissioners, for Hearing, Trying and Adjudging cases of Piracy, Robbery and Felony committed on the High Sea, or within the Admirals Jurisdiction, the said Simon Van Vorst, John Brown, Thomas South, Thomas Baker, Hendrick Quintor, Peter Cornelius Hoof, and John Shuan, all and each of them ought to be punished by Sentence of the said Court with the pains of Death, and loss of Lands, Goods and Chattels, according to the direction of the Law, and for an Example and Terror to all others.

Ja. Smith, Adv[s]. Fis.

The Indictment being Read, the Kings Advocate Moved the Court, That the Prisoners at the Bar should immediately plead Guilty or not Guilty, Alledging that the Statute so directed, and likewise the Civil Law. But Simon Van Vorst for himself & the rest of the Prisoners at the Bar, prayed the Court, That they might have the benefit of Council, before they pleaded, that so they might be well advised what to do. Which request the Court was pleased to Grant. Then they moved, That Mr. Auchmuty should be of Council for them; to which the Court Agreed.

Mr. Auchmuty being admitted, offered some Pleas to the Jurisdiction of the Court: And after a short hearing, the following Questions were propounded by the Prosecutors for the King, and submitted to the Courts Determination. Viz.

Q. 1. Whether the Prisoners shall have liberty allowed them to plead against the Jurisdiction of this Court?

Q. 2. Whether the Prisoners Pleas against the Courts Jurisdiction (if allowed to be made) shall come on before they plead Guilty or not Guilty? And both the said Questions were Voted in the Affirmative.

Then it was alledged and pretended in behalf of the Prisoners, That the Commission of the late Queen Anne was of no force after Her Majesty's Demise: And so the Court had no Power to act by vertue of the said Commission, It having dyed with the Queen: And several Authorities in the Law were Cited and Insisted upon by the Prisoners Council to Maintain his Pleas and Allegations.

To which it was answered, That the Proclamation of His present Majesty King GEORGE, for Continuing Officers, and the subsequent Commission, and the Instructions from the Crown lately Transmitted to the Governour, referring to the Pirates was a sufficient justification of the Authority of the Court to proceed, act, adjudg and determine in all things according to the Powers and Authorities of the above-mentioned Act, which was still in full force; and that the cases which had been Cited, were not to the purpose; and thereupon the following Question was humbly referred to the Courts judgment. Viz.

Quest. Whether this Court hath a sufficient proper Jurisdiction & Trial of the Prisoners at the Bar To which the Court Declared their Opinion in the Affirmative, Nemine Contradicente.

And then all the Prisoners held up their hands again at the Bar, and severally pleaded, Not Guilty, Except John Shuan a French-man, who made known to the Court, That he did not understand English, and therefore was ignorant of what he was charged with in the Indictment. And thereupon Mr. Peter Lucy of Boston, Merchant (being a person of good Credit) was Sworn Interpreter between the Court and the said Shuan; and then by the Courts direction the said Lucy informed the said John Shuan in his own Language of the several Articles Alledged against him in the said Indictment, and then he held up his hand at the Bar and pleaded, Not Guilty.

The Prisoners having severally pleaded to the Indictment, desired Copies thereof, and a further day to prepare for their Trial.

The Court accordingly Ordered the Register without delay to serve the Prisoners with Seven several Copies of the Indictment, with the Names of the Kings Witnesses annexed: And also to issue out Citations to the Witnesses to appear at the next Adjournment. And then the Prisoners were sent back to Goal, and the Court was Adjourned to Tuesday the 22d. day of October, Instant, at Nine of the Clock Ante Meridiem.

At a Justiciary Court of Admiralty held in the Court House in Boston, for and within His Majesty's Province of the Massachusetts-Bay in New England by Adjournment on Tuesday the 22d. of October, Anno Dom. 1717. by His Majesty's Commissioners especially Appointed & Cited, as the Law Directs, to Try, Hear and Adjudge Cases of Piracy, Robbery and Felony Committed on the High Seas, viz.

His Excellency Samuel Shute Esq Governour, Vice Admiral, &c. President. The Honourable William Dummer Esq Lieutenant Governour. The Honourable Elisha Hutchinson, Penn Townsend, Andrew Belcher, John Cushing, Nathaniel Norden, John Wheelwright, BenjaminLynde, Thomas Hutchinson, and Thomas Fitch, Esqrs of His Majesty's Council for this Province. John Meinzies Esq Judge of the Vice Admiralty. Capt. Thomas Smart Commander of His Majesty's Ship of War the Squirrel, John Jekyll Esq Collector of the Plantation Duties.

THe Court being Opened and Proclamation made, Silence was Commanded; And then Elisha Hutchinson and Penn Townsend Esqrs; Two of

His Majesty's Council and Commissioners, being Sworn according to the Statute, took their Places on the Bench.

No Objection being made, by or in behalf of the Prisoners why their Trial should not proceed immediately: the Indictment was again Read.

The Kings Advocate observed to the Prisoners now at the Bar, That if they had anything to say or alledge against the Indictment, It was then their proper time to do it. And there-upon their Procurator urged that one Thomas Davis a Prisoner in BostonGaol might be brought into Court, and allowed to give Evidence in behalf of the Prisoners; And to that end pray'd that their Trial might be deferred till the said Davis could be had to give Evidence for them. Which Motion was rejected by the Court, upon several Authorities urged by the Advocate Gen. shewing, That the said Davis could not lawfully be admitted a Witness for the Prisoners, he being accused of, and tho' not Indicted, yet in Custody for the same Crimes which they stand charged with. And so the Court Resolved to proceed to the Trial of the Prisoners at the Bar without further delay; And then their Procurator Resigned that Trust. Where-upon the Advocate Gen, made a Speech to the Court, to the following Effect.

May it please Your Excellency,

THe Prisoners at the Bar stand Arraigned for sundry Acts of Piracy, Robbery and Felony by them committed at the time and place, and in manner set forth in the Articles of their Indictment, to which they have severally pleaded Not Guilty. It is therefore my duty, in order to convict them of the heinous crimes, they are charged with, to shew first, that the facts laid in the Indictment amount to Piracy, Robbery and Felony; and secondly, that they are all and each of them guilty of these facts;

And if it shall plainly appear to your Excellency & the Honourable, His Majesty's Commissioners now in Court Assembled, that both these points are proved by the strongest and most convincing Evidence, that a case of this Nature can admit of, I doubt not, but from a deep and awful sense of Your duty to God and the King, and a zealous just concern for the common rights and interest of Mankind, the safety of His Majesty's good Subjects in these remote parts, the Preservation and Security of their Trade, the Reputation of this

Colony, and the honour of your Excellency's wise and happy Administration, You will Unanimously concur in Attainting & Condemning them to suffer the Punishment, which the Law requires, and their crimes most justly deserve.

Though the word, Pirate, in its proper & genuine Signification, implies no more than a Seafaring Person, it having been first invented and used by a People, I mean the Greeks, who in early and barbarous Ages, long before Solon and Lycurgus had contrived their Laws, or Athens had become the Seat of Learning, thought it not only lawful but honourable to practice Piracies and Depredations within their Seas, , yet the Laws of all Nations, that have settled into regular Governments, define & declare a Pirate to be an Enemy of Mankind.

And therefore he can claim the Protection of no Prince, the privilege of no Country, the benefit of no Law; He is denied common humanity, and the very rights of Nature, with whom no Faith, Promise nor Oath is to be observed, nor is he to be otherwise dealt with, than a wild & savage Beast, which every Man may lawfully destroy. Quippe adversus Latrones, & c i. e. All persons by the right they have to preserve Mankind in general may and ought to draw the Sword against Robbers, with whom Men can have no Society nor Security. Every one, that findeth me, shall slay me, is the voice of Nature, that the sense of guilt must needs force from such impious Wretches, who have renounced the rights of Nature and Society, and declared themselves to live in opposition to the rules of Equity and Reason, which is the measure set to the Actions of Men for their Mutual Support and Preservation. And to finish the hateful character of this Monster, He is perhaps the only Criminal on Earth, whose crime cannot be absolutely pardoned, nor his punishment remitted by any Prince or State whatever. For as a Pirate is equally an Enemy and dangerous to all Societies, the bonds, which are to secure them from violence and injury, being by him slighted & broken, every Power has equally a right to insist upon Reparation and his being Punished. It is true, Princes are not answerable by the Laws of Nations for Spoils and Robberies committed by their Subjects on those of other Princes, unless they knew and consented to the same, but they are expressly obliged by these Laws, and generally by their own Treaties, to punish or deliver up to be punished such Offenders, and their neglect or refusal will justify a declaration of War, whereof many instances are to be met with in History.

Now as Piracy is in its self a complication of Treason, Oppression, Murder, Assassination, Robbery and Theft, so it denotes the Crime to be perpetrated on the High Sea, or some part thereof, whereby it becomes more Atrocious,

First, Because it is done in remote and Solitary Places, where the weak and Defenceless can expect no Assistance nor Relief; and where these ravenous Beasts of Prey may ravage undisturb'd, hardned in their Wickedness with hopes of Impunity, and of being Concealed forever from the Eyes and Hands of avenging Justice. One of the most aggravating Circumstances, that attend a Crime, is the facility of its being committed, that is, where the Malefactor cannot easily be prevented nor discovered.

Thus by the Law of GOD Theft in the Field was more grievously Punished, than Theft in a House. And he that lay in wait for his Neighbour and slew him, was to be forced from the Sanctuary & put to Death without Pity. By the Roman Law every secret attempt on a mans Life by Assassination, Poison or other ways is Punished Capitally. So is Stealing Cloaths in places for Bathing. And both by that and the Divine Law a Night Thief may lawfully be Kill'd. Ea sunt animadvertenda peccota Maxime, que difficillime precavcntur. i. e. Those Crimes ought to be Punished with the utmost Severity, which cannot without the greatest difficulty be prevented.

Another Aggravation of this Crime is, That the unhappy Persons on whom it is acted, are the most Innocent in themselves, and the most Useful and Beneficial to the Publick; whose indefatigable Industry conveys amidst innumerable Dangers, besides that of falling into the hands of Pirates, Blood into the Veins of the Body Politick, and nourishes every Member. Ships are under the Publick Care, Interest Reip. Us ••ves exercean•ur, i. e. It is the Interest of the State, that Shipping be improved. And to this Improvement our Nation owes its Greatness, Safety and Riches. Masters of Ships are Publick Officers, and therefore every Act of Violence and Spoliation committed on them or their Ships, may justly be accounted Treason, and so it was before the Statute of the 25th of Edward III.

The Third Circumstance, which blackens exceedingly and augments a

Pirates Guilt, is the Danger, wherewith every State or Government is threatned from the Combinations, Conspiracies and Confederacies of Profligate and Desperate Wretches, united by no other tie (for what other can there be among such?) than a mutual Consent to extinguish first Humanity in themselves, and to Prey promiscuously on all others. Ni•••m grassanti••es, opus ost Example. Hannibal's Victorious Army was never more terrible to Rome, than that of Spartacus, who in three set Battles shook the power of that Mighty Empire, flew their Consuls, and cut down the flower of Italy. Pompey by his Successful management of the War against the Pirates in his time obtained the Glorious Sir-name of Great, a Mark of Honour, to which none of his former Victories and Triumphs (tho' these were more, sayes the Oratour, Quam cateri l•gerunt had advanced his Merit, nor any Roman General before him had aspired: And yet after all, the Pirates were reduced rather by Treaties and Concessions, than subdued by the power of Pompey's Army. I presume there are few, who do not know that the Pirates on the coast of Barbary, after many Devastations and Robberies committed by them at Sea, and on the Christian Shoar, at last in Spite of the most vigorous opposition, the greatest Princes of Europe were able to make, formed themselves into Governments, and erected Kingdoms, which even to this time prove the bane and plague of Christendom.

But I need not go far to find out instances of this kind. It was but the other day we saw and felt with horrour the formidable power of such confederated Villains, who increasing in Strength in proportion to the number of their Crimes, & by every repeated act of cruelty being inabled to commit a greater, dared at last not only to infest our Coasts, seize our Ships, & put a full stop to our Commerce, but to enter our Harbours, and if Providence had not raised the Winds & Waves for our deliverance, who can say, but these vile Remains of that abominable Crew, reserved in a wonderful manner for Publick Justice, that others may be amended and deter'd by their example, might have been now giving Laws to those, from whom they expect to receive their doom.

Having offered to your Excellency this short and imperfect view of the Nature and Effects of Piracy in General, I beg leave in the next Place to observe briefly from the Principles of the Civil Law, which is appointed to rule and direct the proceedings of this Honourable Court, what Acts do necessarily infer the guilt and penalty of that Crime.

The first Act consists in the mind, animus depradandi, and if it rests there only, it cannot fall under the censure of any humane Judicature; for as no Person can receive prejudice by Acts meerly internal, it cannot reasonably be supposed to be the interest or concern of any to have one punished for them. But when these inward motions come to discover themselves by undoubted tokens, and break out in some open Act, tho' that proceeds no farther, than an endeavour or bare attempt, yet the Guilt and Punishment are the same, as if the intended mischief had been fully executed. Consilia Hominum non eventa legibus vindicanture. i. e. The vengeance of the Laws levelled at the designs and intentions of Men, and not the events of things. To the same purpose is the Emperour Hadrians Rescript, In Malesicijs voluntas Spectatur non exitus. i. e. The weight and importance of every Offence must be measured by the Malefactors Will and not success of the Action. Et paritur paccandi sola voluntas. For the Law considers every crime as actually accomplished, with respect to the Guilt, tho' the Fact be not committed. Omnia scelera etiam ante effectum operis, quantum culpa satis est perfecta sunt.

The Man, for instance, who goes armed on purpose to assassinate or rob, mixes poison to give to another, sollicites the chastity of a Married Woman, attempts to Steal, to corrupt another's Servant, to betray his Country is in the eye of the Law no less an Assassin or Robber, a Poisoner, an Adulterer, a Thief, a Corruptor, a Traitor, than if he had succeeded in the Attempt, and effectually compleated his design. And consequently the attacking, invading or entering a free Ship, Animo depredandi, the attempting to Rob or Steal the goods on board, the offering violence to the Master or his Crew or putting them under restraint, are so many direct acts of Piracy tho' there be no capture nor taking, nor any damage done, and the Aggressour, if he is overcome and taken on the High Sea, may be lawfully hang'd up at the Yard-Arm, it being permitted to every Man to use in such cases his natural Liberty, where no Judicature can be applied to for redress.

It is otherwise at Common Law, and I wish the nature of the Prisoners Guilt were such, as to leave the least room for considering the difference of the Laws in this point. How many Innocent lives had been saved, how many Families preserved from extream Misery and Ruin? Heaven has suffered them to prevail in their Attempts, and to pursue their execrable designs to the last degree of Wickedness.

Their own Confessions, emitted before your Excellency, open a dreadful scene of Depredations, Robberies and barbarous Cruelties, exercised by them before they came on this Coast, where, to fill up the measure of their Guilt, they committed the Crimes, for which they are now Indicted, Namely, That on the 26th of April last they surprized and with Force and Arms entered a Vessel belonging to His Majesty's Subjects in Ireland, and having subdued the Master and his Crew and made themselves Masters of the Vessel and Cargo, they forced the Master with five of his hands (there being in all eight on Board) to abandon his Vessel and to go on board the Piratical Ship Whido, where soon after they perished in the Shipwreck.

And in this respect, tho' the Prisoners are not charged with Murder in the Articles of their Indictment, yet I may justly affirm on the best Authorities in Law, that they are truly Murtherers. Nibil interest, Occidat quis, an cansane Mortis prabeat. They Robb'd the Cargo and Goods on board, and Navigated the Vessel in company with their Accomplices, who were then possessed of several Ships and Vessels under the Command of their Capital Ship the Whido, in order to carry Destruction to the utmost parts of our Territories. The bare naming of these Facts is enough to prove the first point, viz. That the Facts laid in the Indictment amount to Piracy, &c. That the Prisoners are all and each of them Guilty of these Facts will evidently appear to your Excellency from the Testimonies of three Persons, who belonged to the Vessel, and were detained on Board after the Master and five more were turned away.

And albeit the law presumes every Act of Piracy to be habitual, yet that in Fact they have long ago given themselves up to such a Flagitious course of Life, several worthy and credible Persons will testify and declare. The Witnesses are here in Court, and I humbly move that they may be examined and interrogated on the several Articles of the Indictment

Then the Witnesses for the King were called into Court, and the Prisoners were asked if they had any just Challenge or Objection to make against them; but none being offered, the Witnesses were severally Sworn in order following, Viz.

THomas Fitz Gyrald late Mate of the Pink Mary Anne of Dublin in Ireland, Testifyeth and saith, That on or about the Twenty-fourth day of April last past, the said Pink lest Nantasket in New-England, bound for New York, under Command of Capt. Andrew Crumpstey; and on Friday the 26th day of the said Month, between the Hours of Four & Six of the Clock in the Morning, they discovered two Sail a-Stern, viz. a large Ship and a Snow, between Nantucket Shoals & St. Georges Banks, which came up with the Pink in the Morning, with the Kings Ensign and Pendant flying; the large Ship was found to be the Whido, whereof Samuel Bellamy a Pirate was Commander, Who ordered the Pink to strike her Colours, and then hoisted out their Boat, and sent the Seven Prisoners, now at the Bar, on board the said Pink, all Armed with Musquets, Pistols and Cutlashes, except Thomas South and John Shuan. And further the Deponent, Declares & saith, That the said Thomas South, soon after he came on board, Declared to him the Deponent his Intention to make his escape from the Whido, as soon as he could, but Shuan was very forward active on board the Pink, altho' he had no Weapon with him.

That Thomas Baker went to the said Capt. Crumpstey with his Sword drawn, and ordered him to go on board the said Ship with all his Papers, and five of his hands, who were forced to obey, and accordingly Rowed on board the said Ship Whido in the Boat, while the Seven Pirates now at the Bar tarryed on board the Pink with the Deponent, and Alexander Mackconachy & James Dunavan. And in a little time after several more Men came from the Ship on board the Pink for some Wine, but finding it difficult to be come at, returned to their own Ship, with a small quantity of Wine and some Cloaths which belonged to the Ships Company. And soon after the Boat was again hoisted into the Ship, from whence he hail'd the Pink and gave orders to the Prisoners now at the Bar (who had forcibly taken Command of her) to Steer North-West and by North; Who answered, They would, and accordingly followed that Course, till about Four of the Clock in the afternoon, when the Ship and the Snow, which last was also taken and made a Prize of by

Capt. Bellamy, and the Pink lay too, it being very thick, foggy Weather. And presently after the Snow came under the Ships Stern, and told Capt. Bellamy, They had made discovery of Land. Wherefore he ordered the Pink to Steer away North, which the Prisoners did; And when Night came on the Ship put out a Light a-Stern, as well as the Snow and the Pink: And also a Sloop from Virginia surprized and taken by Capt. Bellamy the same day; and then all of them made Sail again.

The Deponent further saith, That Capt. Bellamy Commanded the said Simon Van Vorst and Company on board the Pink to make more haste: Whereupon John Brown Swore, That he would carry Sail till she carryed her Masts away. That when the Deponent & Mackconachy were Prisoners, Simon Van Vorst told Mackconachy, That if he would not find Liquor he would break his Neck. Thomas Baker said they had got a Commission from King George, and Simon Van Vorst answered, We will stretch it to the Worlds end. The Prisoners at the Bar Drank plentifully of the Wine on board the Pink that day they took her; went to the Helm by turns and had the government of the Pink; and some of them ordered the Deponent to help to reef the Topsail, and do other services; She proved Leaky, so all hands were forced to Pump hard, and therefore they Damn'd the Vessel and wished they had never seen her.

The Prisoners Van Vorst, Baker and Brown with the Deponent, were divided into two Watches, and about Ten a Clock at Night the Weather grew so thick, it Lightned and Rained hard, and was so very dark that the Pinks Company could not see the Shoar till they were among the Breakers: When the Deponent was at Helm, and had lost sight of the Pirate Ship, Snow and Sloop, and discerning that they were among the Breakers; they were about to trim the Head sail, but before they could do it the Pink run a-shore, opposite to Slutts-bush, so called, to the South-ward of Cape Cod, between Ten and Eleven a Clock at Night, about which time the Prisoners at the Bar or some of them (being fearful as the Deponent supposed lest they should be Apprehended on Shoar) Cryed out saying, For God's sake let us go down into the Hould & Die together.

And the whole pinks Company tarry'd on Board her all that Night: And in their Distress the Prisoners ask'd the Deponent to Read to them the Common-Prayer Book, which he did about an Hour; And at break of Day they found the shoar-side of the Pink dry, so all of them jumpt out upon an Island, where they tarryed till about Ten a Clock, and eat Sweetmeats and other things taken out of a Chest, which Quintor and Shuan broke open, and drank of the Wines which came out of the Pink: About which time two Men, viz. John Cole and William Smith came over to the Island in a Cannoe, and carry'd the Pinks Company to the Main Land; and then Mackconachy discovered the Pirates, so that they were Apprehended by Warrant from Mr. Justice Doan at Eastham, from whence they were brought to Boston Gaol.

The Deponent further saith, That while they were on the Island, Brown and others would have him call himself Captain of the Pink, and give out that the Pirates on Board were his Men: and after the Prisoners had got on the Main Land they talked in divers Languages, and were in a great hurry to go to Rhode-Island the better to make their Escape, as the Deponent imagines.

JAmes Dunavan Mariner, late belonging to the Pink Mary Anne, and Brother-in-Law to Captain Crumpstey late Master thereof saith, That the said Pink belonged to Ireland, was Owned by the Subjects of the King of Great-Britain, and was Taken on the 26th Day of April last past, under English Colours by Samuel Bellamy Commander of the Pirate Ship Whido, That Simon Van Vorst and the rest of the Prisoners at the Bar came on Board the Pink Armed, and had their Pistols Charged with Powder and Ball, except Thomas South and John Shuan, and Ordered the Captain, with Five Hands more to go on Board the Ship with his Papers: And that the Prisoners at the Bar steer'd the Pink after Bellamy's Ship, as he gave Orders.

That they drank plentifully of the Wines on Board; That Thomas South's Behaviour in the Pink was civil and peaceable. The Deponent further saith, That he heard John Baker threaten to shoot Mackconachy, Cook of the Pink, thro' the head, because he steer'd to the windward of his Course; and said moreover, That he would make no more to shoot him, than he would a Dog; and that he should never go on shoar to tell his Story. That one of the Prisoners asked the Deponent what he thought they were? To which Baker, who stood by, said, That the King had given them a Commission to make their Fortune, and they were sworn to do it. After the Pink was cast on shoar, they said, They were in as bad a condition then as before.

ALexander Mackconachy, late Cook of the Pink Mary Anne of Dublin, saith, That on the 26th day of April last past, in the course of their Voyage from Nantasket to New-York, they were taken by a Pirate Ship called the Whido, Commanded by Capt. Samuel Bellamy, That all the Prisoners at the Bar came on Board the said Pink armed, except Thomas South and John Shuan, and made themselves Masters of the Pink; and that Simon Van Vorst ordered the Captain to go on board the Ship Whido, with his Papers and five of his hands. The Deponent further saith, That the Pink was cast away opposite to an Island, called Slutts-bush; and after the Prisoners were carryed to the Main Land they looked very sorrowful, and made all imaginable speed in order to escape from the hands of Justice. That Thomas South behaved himself Civily. That Thomas Baker cut down the Fore-mast & Mizen-mast of the pink when she run on shoar.

JOhn Brett Mariner, Testifyeth and saith, That in the Month of June 1716. he was taken by two Pirate Sloops, one Commanded by Capt. Samuel Bellamy, and the other by Capt. Labous; They Damn'd the Deponent, and bid him bring his Liquor on board; they carryed him to the Island of Pynes, and he was detained a Prisoner by them there Eighteen days; During which time John Brown was as active on board the Pirate Sloop as the rest of the Company: He told a Prisoner then on board, that he would hide him in the Hold, and hinder him from complaining against him, or telling his Story.

THomas Checkley Mariner saith, That he knows John Shuan the Prisoner at the Bar, That he belonged to the Tanner Frigot one John Stouer Master, and sometime in March last the said Ship or Frigot was taken in the prosecution of her Voyage from pettyguavus to Old France, by Capt. Samuel Bellamy and Monsieur Lebous, they pretended to be Robbin Hoods Men. That Shuan declared himself to be now a Pirate and went up and unrigged the Main top-mast by order of the Pirates, who at that time forced no Body to go with them; and said they would take no Body against their Wills.

MOses Norman says, That he knows Thomas Brown, and saw him in company with the Pirates belonging to Capt. Bellamy, & Monsieur Labous when the Deponent was taken with Capt. Brett in the Month of June, 1716. That he was carryed to the Isle of Pynes, and kept Prisoner Seventeen or Eighteen days, during all which time the said Thomas Brown was very active on board of Capt. Labous.

JOhn Cole saith, That on the Twenty-seventh day of April last he saw the Prisoners now at the Bar, in Eastham soon after they were cast on shore, That they tarryed a short time at his house, and look'd very much dejected and cast down; they enquired the way to Rhode-Island, and made great haste from his house, tho' he asked them to tarry and refresh themselves.

JOhn Done Esq saith, That hearing there were some pirates journeying towards Rhode-Island, he pursued them with a Deputy Sheriff and other Assistants, and seized the Prisoners now at the Bar at Eastham Tavern about the 27th of April last; When they confessed that they belonged to Capt. Bellamy Commander of the Ship Whido, and had taken the Pink Mary Anne in which they run on shoar.

After the afore-named Witnesses were examined, the Court in favour of the Prisoners by giving them time to make their Defence, Adjourned till three a Clock Post Meridiem.

The Court met about that time, and the Prisoners were sent for & brought again to the Bar. When the President observed to them, That this Court had given them time, till now, to make their own Defence; Then demanded what they had to say for themselves.

Simon Van Vorst alledged, That he was forced by Capt. Bellamy's Company to do what he did, and would have made known his intentions to make his escape from the Pirates unto the Mate of the said Pink, but that he understood by the Mates discourse that he inclined to be a Pirate himself; and therefore he did not discover his Mind to the Mate.

Thomas Brown pretended himself also to be a forced Man but produced no Evidence to make it appear to the Court.

Thomas South alledged, That he belonged to a Bristol Ship, whereof one James Williams was Master; That he was taken by Capt. Bellamy, and forced to carry with him, otherwise was threatened to be put upon a desolate Island, where there was nothing to support him.

Thomas Baker saith, That he and Simon Van Vorst were both taken out of one Vessel; That he attempted to make his escape at Spanish Town, and the Governour of that Place seemed to favour his design, till Capt. Bellamy and his Company sent the Governour word that they would burn & destroy the Town, if that the said Baker, and those that concealed themselves with him were not delivered up. And afterwards he would have made his escape at Crab Island, but was hindered by four of Capt. Bellamy's Company.

Hendrick Quintor saith, That he was taken by Capt. Bellamy and Monsieur Labous, and they had agreed to let him go to the Coast of Crocus in the French Vessel which they took him in, but the Commander thereof soon after dyed, and so Capt. Bellamy would not permit him to proceed the said Voyage, and he was unavoidably forced to continue among the Pirates.

Peter Cornelius Hoof declares and saith, That he was taken by Capt. Bellamy in a Vessel whereof John Cornelius was Master, That the said Bellamy's Company Swore they would kill him unless he would joyn with them in their Unlawful Designs.

John Shuan by his Interpreter saith, That he was sick at the time when Capt. Bellamy took him, and went on board the Pirate Vessel at the Instance of Capt. Bellamy's Doctor, who advised him to stay with him till his Cure. And that when he went on board the Pink Mary Anne he did not carry any Arms with him; and that he hoped by going on board the Pink he should the sooner make his escape from the Pirates, for that he had a better way of getting his living than by Pirating.

THE Evidences for the King being fully heard, and also the Pleas & Allegations made by the Prisoners at the Bar; His Majesty's Attorney General in a very handsome and learned Speech summed up the Evidence, and made his Remarks upon the whole; and after him the Advocate General having resumed the Articles of Indictment, the Depositions of Witnesses, and the Prisoners defences, observed to the Court, That their pretence of being forced out of the respective Ships and Vessels, they belonged to, by Bellamy and Labous, if it was true, can never excuse their Guilt, Since no case of Necessity can justify a direct violation of the Divine and Moral Law, and give one the liberty of Sinning, whatever exceptions may be allowed from Laws purely

Possitive, and humane establishments: But on the contrary, that they acted freely and by their own choice, is most plain and obvious, for when they had the fairest opportunity, that could have happen'd, to make their escape, if they had intended it, by means of the Weather, Wind and nearness of the Shoar, they were obstinately resolved rather to hazard the Vessel and their Lives, than lose company with the Whido.

That Shuan and Souths going on board the Pink unarmed, is not material, nor does that circumstance extenuate the Crime in the least; if the rest had gone without Arms, as they might with security enough, considering their Number, and the weak condition of those, they had to deal with, and that the Pink then lay under Bellamy's command, Can any Person imagine they would have been less criminal?

Suppose one or two Ruffians having no Arms meet a Man in the Highway, and instead of threatening and force, give him good Words, and at the same time put their hands in his Pockets and rob him of his Money, Are they not to be accounted Robbers because they did not draw a Sword or Pistol? The guilt is incurred by possessing the Innocent Persons mind with such just apprehensions and dread of extream danger, as to determine him to avoid a greater evil by exposing himself to a less one that is to save his Life by delivering up his goods. That it appears evidently by the Deposition of Checkley, that Shuan at the time they both belonged to one Vessel voluntarily joyned the Pirates, and the three first Witnesses declare, That he acted his part on board the Pink with as much forwardness as the rest.

That as to Souths inoffensive behaviour on board, and his inclination to make his escape, it shews the pressure of his guilt, but does not take off the weight in the eye of the Law. He was a part of the Crew, marked in the Watch Roll, intituled to a share of the booty, and imployed in such interprizes, as none but experienced and accomplished Villains could have been trusted with, and tho' at last perhaps he might not seem so active as the rest, yet his very presence on board the Pink involved him in the same crime, and Facinus, quos inquinat, AEquat. Besides, it being proved by the Oaths of some of the Witnesses, That Bellamy and Labous did not press anybody (nor indeed is it credible they would) and there being no reason to doubt of his listing himself amongst those, with whom we found him, his Repentance may save his Soul, but cannot except him from the punishment due to his crime: It being a Maxim both in Law and Morality, That an involuntary act taking its rise from an act that is voluntary, is likewise accounted voluntary.

And as it hath ever been the glory of our August Monarchs to suppress Piracies by force & wholesome Laws, whilst other Nations have to their perpetual disgrace called Pirates to their assistance and admitted them to a share of the Plunder. As the English Trade is in the utmost danger at present in America from the prodigious Number of Ships exercised in Piracies, and as Providence hath wonderfully preserved us by destroying their Capital Ship with her Numerous Crew, and hath no less wonderfully delivered into the hands of Publick Justice, the Prisoners at the Bar, to teach others by their Exemplary Punishment to abhor the barbarous and inhumane practices, which have been fully proved against them, and whereof they stand convicted.

He humbly moved His Excellency and the Honourable the Commissioners to proceed to pass Sentence of Death upon all and each of them, they being all equally Guilty; and concluded with saying, That to shew the least Pity in matters of this Kind, where the Proofs are so full and Pregnant, and not the least presumption in favour of the Prisoners, would be the greatest cruelty. Unnum Pietatis genus, in hac re esse crudelem.

The Court was Cleared, and the Evidences and Pleadings there upon against the Prisoners, with their Defences, having been duly considered, and the Question put with respect to each of the Prisoners severally, Guilty or not Guilty. The Court Voted Simon Van Vorst, John Brown, Thomas Baker, Hendrick Quintor, Peter Cornelius Hoof, and John Shuan, Guilty of Piracy, Robbery, and Felony, according to the Indictment.

But forasmuch as Thomas South at the time when the Pink Mary Anne was taken, went on board her without Arms in a Peaceable manner; and manifested and declared unto Fitz Gyrald the Mate of the Pink when she was in sight of the Ship Whido and there was no sufficient grounds to hope for his escape, That he was taken from on board of a Jamaica Vessel and compelled utterly against his Will to joyn with the Pirates; And that he was fully resolved to leave them the first opportunity that should afterwards present, and his

Behaviour and Carriage towards the Mate being always Civil and Kind; The Court were opinion, and accordingly Voted, That Thomas South is Not Guilty.

Then the Prisoners were brought again to the Bar, and severally asked, (except Thomas South) Whether they had anything further to say why Sentence of Death should not be Pronounced against them according to Law. And nothing being offered, more than what was said upon their Trial, by any of them, except John Brown; who pleaded the benefit of Clergy, which was denyed him, being contrary to Law; The President Pronounced the Decree of the Court against the said Simon Van Vorst, John Brown, Thomas Baker, Hendrick Quintor, Peter Cornelius Hoof, and John Shuan in the words following. Viz.

THis Court having duly considered the Indictment & the Proofs of the several Articles contained therein, together with your Defences, Have found you Simon Van Vorst, John Brown, Thomas Baker, Hendrick Quintor, Peter Cornelius Hoof, and John Shuan, Guilty, of the Crimes of Piracy, Robbery and Felony, as is set forth in the Indictment, And do therefore Adjudge and Decree, That you Simon Van Vorst, John Brown, Thomas Baker, Hendrick Quintor, Peter Cornelius Hoof, and John Shuan, shall go hence to the Place from whence you came, and from thence you shall be carried to the Place of Execution, and there you and each of you, shall be hanged up by the Neck until you & each of you are Dead; And the Lord have Mercy on your Souls.

And the Court do also ordain, That all your Lands, Tenements, Goods and Chattles be forfeited to the King, and brought into His Majesty's use.

President. Thomas South, The Court have found you not Guilty: Whereupon he put himself upon his Knees and Thanked the Court, &c. And after he was duly Admonished and had Promised Amendment of Life, &c. he was Dismist, and taken out of the Bar.

Then Charge was given to the Sheriffs to take special Care of the Condemned Prisoners, and the Court was Adjourned till Monday the 28th of October Currant at Nine a Clock in the Forenoon.

The Sentence was accordingly executed by Mr. Vincent Marshal of the Court of Admiralty, the Sheriffs assisting, on the 15th day of November following at Charlestown Ferry within flux and reflux of the Sea.

The Trial of Thomas Davis

At a Justiciary Court of Admiralty held in the Court House in Boston, for and within His Majesty's Province of the Massachusetts-Bay in New England by Adjournment on Monday the 28th. of October, 1717. by His Majesty's Commissioners especially Appointed & Cited, as the Law Directs, to Try, Hear and Adjudge Cases of Piracy, Robbery and Felony Committed on the High Seas, viz.

His Excellency Samuel Shute Esq Governour, Vice Admiral, &c. President. The Honourable William Dummer Esq Lieutenant Governour. The Honourable Elisha Hutchinson, Penn Townsend, John Cushing, Thomas Hutchinson, and Thomas Fitch, Esqrs of His Majesty's Council for this Province. John Meinzies Esq Judge of the Vice Admiralty. Capt. Thomas Smart Commander of His Majesty's Ship of War the Squirrel, John Jekyll Esq Collector of the Plantation Duties.

THE Court being Opened by Proclamation issued out a Warrant Directed to the Sheriffs of Suffolk, Requiring them forthwith to bring into Court the Body of Thomas Davis from His Majesty's Goal in Boston, where he was Committed, being accused of Piracy, Robbery and Felony on the High Seas; and accordingly the Sheriffs brought the said Thomas Davis to the Bar of this Court: When Silence was Commanded, and after he was Arraigned, and the Indictment filed against him by His Majesty's Advocate, for the Crimes aforesaid was Read, and is as follows. Viz.

The Preamble the same as in the Indictment before.

I. ANd first, The said Thomas Davis, sometime about the latter end of February, or beginning of March last past, did in Confederacy, Combination, and Conspiracy with divers other Profligate & Felonious Persons, without any lawful Cause or Warrant, in hostile manner, with force and Arms, Piratically, and Feloniously, chase, assault, invade & enter, on the High Sea, Viz. in the Windward Passage, about three Leagues off the Island commonly called Long-Island in the West Indies, a Free Trading Ship called the Whido, bound from His Majesty's Colony of Jamaica, to the Port of London, which Ship then was Owned and Navigated by His Majesty's Subjects, of Great Britain, having her own Cargoe on board, and displaying English Colours.

II. And secondly, The said Thomas Davis, having at the time and place, and in manner aforesaid entered on board the said Ship, did then and there in Confederacy, Combination, and Conspiracy, with divers other Profligate and Felonious Persons, Piratically and Feloniously over-power, subdue and imprison, Lawrence Prince Master of the said Ship, and his Crew, and him the said Lawrence Prince, with his said Crew, did force and constrain, to leave and abandon the said Ship, and her Cargoe, consisting chiefly of Sugar, Indigo, Jesuits Bark, Silver and Gold.

III. Thirdly, The said Thomas Davis, at the time and place aforesaid, in Confederacy, Combination, and Conspiracy, with divers other profligate and Felonious Persons, Piratically and Feloniously seized and possessed himself of the said Ship and Cargoe; and the said Ship did use, navigate, exercise and imploy in Confederacy with others aforesaid, in Perpetrating and Committing Piracies, Robberies and Depredations.

IV. Fourthly, The said Thomas Davis sometime about the latter end of March or beginning of April last past, then being on board the said Piratical Ship aforesaid, Did on the High Sea, viz. off or near the Capes of Virginia, in Confederacy, Combination and Conspiracy with other Profligate and Felonious Persons, Piratically and Feloniously surprize, assault and take a Free trading Vessel bound from His Majesty's Colony of Barbadoes, to some part of Great Britain, which Vessel then belonged to and was Navigated by His Majesty's Subjects of that part of Great Britain called Scotland, having on board her own Cargoe.

V. Fifthly, The said Thomas Davis at the time and place aforesaid, Did in Confederacy, Combination and Conspiracy with divers other Profligate and

Felonious Persons, Piratically and Feloniously, seize and imprison the Master & Crew belonging to the said Vessel, and Robbed the Cargoe thereof, and the said Vessel then and there, and in manner aforesaid, did sink and destroy.

All which Facts of Piracy, Robbery and Felony having been done, perpetrated and committed at the several times and places, and in manner in the preceeding Articles specified and set forth by the said Thomas Davis; And he being thereof duly Convicted and Attainted upon such Accumulative probation offered to be made before His Majesty's Commissioners, in hearing, trying and adjudging cases of Piracy, Robbery and Felony committed on the High Sea, or within the Admirals Jurisdiction, as the discovery of crimes so heinous and atrocious, practised in remote parts, and so Industriously and Obstinately endeavoured to be concealed, admits and requires, he the said Thomas Davis ought to be punished by Sentence of the said Court with the pains of Death, and loss of Lands, Goods and Chattles according to the direction of the Law, to the Example and Terror of others to do, or commit the like crimes in times coming.

Ja. Smith, Adv[1]. Fis.

The Indictment being Read, It was moved to the Court by the Kings Advocate, That the Prisoner should immediately plead Guilty or not Guilty. But the Prisoner humbly moved the Court that he might have Council assigned him, which was allowed. And Mr. Valentine was admitted his Attorney; then the Prisoner held up his hand at the Bar, and pleaded Not Guilty. After which the Court ordered the Register to serve the Prisoner with a Copy of the Indictment, with the Names of the Witnesses annexed; and then Adjourned to Wednesday the 30th of October Currant at Nine a Clock in the forenoon.

At a Justiciary Court of Admiralty held in the Court House at Boston for and within His Majesty's Province of the Massachusetts-Bay in New-England, by Adjournment on Wednesday the 30th day of October, Anno Dom 1717. by His Majesty's Commissioners specially appointed & Cited as the Law directs to try, hear and adjudge cases of Piracy, Robbery and Felony Committed on the High Seas, viz.

His Excellency Samuel Shute, Esq Governour, Vice Admiral, &c. President.

The Hon. William Dummer Esq Lieut. Governour. The Hon. Elisha Hutchinson, Penn Townsend, John Cushing, Nathaniel Paine, John Otis, John Wheelwright, Thomas Fitch, Edmund Quincey, Esqrs of His Majesty's Council for this Province. John Meinzies Esq Judge of the Vice Admiralty, Capt. Thomas Smart Commander of His Majesty's Ship of War the Squirrel, John Jekyll Esq Collector of the Plantation Duties.

Intra.

Thomas Davis.

Mr. Smith Advocate G. Prosecutor.

Mr. Dudley Attorney G.

- Curia Legitime Affirmata, Mr. Valentine, Procurator in Defence.

The Prisoner by order of Court being brought to the Bar, The Kings Advocate moved, That if the Prisoner's Council had any just Objections against the Indictment, that it would be proper to make them before the Witnesses on His Majesty's behalf were examined; but no Objections being offered, he spoke in the manner following.

May it please Your Excellency,

THe Prisoner at the Bar is arraigned before You, for Crimes of Piracy, Robbery and Felony by him committed on the High Sea, in Confederacy, combination and conspiracy with others like himself. i. e. Profligate and Felonious Persons; And has pleaded Not Guilty.

Tho' the Nature of the Proof, that is now offered to be made, is cumulative, yet your Excellency will easily observe, That the Facts to be proved are not so joyned and connected, as to make up and Accumulate the Crime, for take them singly and apart, everyone is a direct and compleat act of Piracy, but are laid down as so many aggravated Circumstances, whereby the Crime becomes more heinous, and the Prisoners guilt proportionably more black and odious.

To attack a Free trading Ship is unquestionably an act of Piracy, and the subsequent Facts, viz. Entering on board, seizing and imprisoning the Master and his Crew, carrying away one Ship & her Cargoe, and robbing the

Cargoe of another, and sinking the Vessel, are so many distinct Supervening Crimes, which differ only according to the several degrees of the wrongs and oppressions, which necessarily flow from thence.

The Evidence, which I shall lay before Your Excellency is of three kinds. 1st By the Prisoners Confession. 2 By Witnesses. 3. By Presumptions called in the Civil Law Argumenta et Indicia. But in regard the practice of Civilians in cases Criminal may be mistaken, or perhaps not well understood in these parts, I beg leave briefly to mention some particulars concerning the Nature of this Evidence, in order to obviate and remove some doubts and objections, which probably may be raised against it.

I. Confession is the strongest and surest proof in Law; according to the Maxim, In confiteniem null• sunt Judicis partis, and the reason is because Confessus pro Judicato habetur. It is true, an extrajudicial Confession is not of that validity and force, but is admitted only under certain Restrictions and limitations, whereof I shall name only three, as being agreed to by all Civilians. 1st. If it is emitted before a Judge competent. 2d. If it is supported by presumptions. 3d. If it is brought to prove the circumstances of a Crime.

II As to Witnesses, I shall only observe, that two Witnesses concurring in their depositions to one and the same Fact, are not required in proving a crime by the Civil Law. If 1st. They are not contrary, but assist one another; As if one should Swear, that he saw a Thief goe in without a Horse, and another saw him take the Horse, and no more; This would be sufficient to convict the Thief. And 2dly. When the Witnesses depone upon different acts in a crime, that is reiterable, as in Adultery, Piracy, and Robbery, and in such cases they are Contestes sufficient for inflicting the pains of Death.

III. The last part of our Evidence is by Presumptions, and that crimes may be proved by Presumptions, is most clear from the Rescript of Valerius, Que Argumenta, &c. i. e. What Arguments are sufficient to prove anything, cannot certainly be determined, I can only therefore injoyn you in short, that in your inquiry and decision, you are not to be tied to any one sort of Proof, but you must judge according to your own Conscience, what you believe to be true, or what you think not sufficiently proved.

And in Atrocious crimes, which by the Civilians are called excepted cases, amongst which Piracy is deservedly reckoned one, where wickedness industriously indeavours to hide itself, It is a constant rule, Probatio per Indicia, &c. i. e. That probation by conjectures and presumptions in things hard to be proved, and secretly committed, is held to be good and evident proof. And to the same purpose, Secus tamen se res habet, &c. i. e. But the matter is otherwise, if many presumptions concur and lead the Defendant, of which anyone may be proved, and by a single Witness; for one presumption strengthens another, and many of them joined together make proof.

It is not necessary that one crime be made evident by one manner of proof only, for several sorts of proof may be so joined, that those which taken alone could not affect the Criminal, yet being put together fall upon his head like a Storm of Hail and overwhelm him.

I shall conclude with that most Excellent constitution of the Emperor Theodosius. Sciant cuncti accusatores, &c. i. e. Let all Prosecutors take notice. That when they bring a Criminal matter into Publick Judgment, it ought to be supported by proper Witnesses, or plain Proofs, or undoubted presumptions, as clear as the Sun.

This is the Rule, which I propose to follow in the course of this Trial, and as I would with great Submission recommend to Your Excellency and the Honourable Bench the wise direction given, Sed nec de Suspicionibus, &c. That no man ought to be condemned on bare Suspicions, for it is better that a guilty man pass Unpunished, than that an Innocent man should be Condemned: So on the other hand, I humbly move, the Nature of the Crime, the Prisoner is charged with and the manner of proof adduced to convict him, may be duely considered, and if his guilt shall plainly appear by his own confession, the evidence of Witnesses, and violent necessary presumptions, that he may by Sentence of this Honourable Court suffer the Punishment, which the Law inflicts.

Then the Kings Evidences were called into Court, and no objections against them being made by the Prisoner.

OWen Morris Mariner was first Examined upon Oath, Who Solemnly Testifyed & Declared, That he knew the Prisoner at the Bar, That he belonged to the Ship St. Michael whereof James Williams was Master; And in the

THE TRIAL OF THOMAS DAVIS

Month of Sept. 1716. they left Bristol bound to Jamaica, & in Decemb. following the said Ship was taken by two Pirate Sloops, one commanded by Capt. Sam Bellamy, & the other by Loues Lebous, about Twenty Leagues off Sabria, That they gave the said Williams his Ship and detained the Prisoner because he was a Carpenter & a Single Man, together with Three others of the Ships company.

And further the Deponent saith, That the Prisoner was very unwilling to go with Bellamy, and prevailed with him by reason of his Intreaties to promise that he should be discharged in the next Vessel that was taken: And afterwards the Deponent was again taken in the Ship Whido, commanded by Capt. Prince by the said Capt. Bellamy, who was then commander of the Ship Sultania, taken from Capt. Richards, as the Deponent understood, and then he saw the Prisoner aboard the said Ship; at which time the Prisoner reminded the said Bellamy of his promise: when he asked him, If he was willing to go, He answered, Yes: and then the said Capt. Bellamy replied, If the company would consent he should go: And thereupon he asked his company, If they were willing to let Davis the Carpenter go? Who expressed themselves in a Violent manner, saying, No, Damn him, they would first shoot him or whip him to Death at the Mast.

Thomas South Mariner, lately taken by Capt. Samuel Bellamy in the Pirate Ship Whido cast away upon this Coast, and discharged upon his Trial, was admitted an Evidence, and being accordingly Sworn, saith, That the said Bellamy while he was in command of the said Ship Whido, took a Scotch Vessel off the Capes of Virginia last Spring, Cut down her Masts & sunk her: That he heard the said Thomas Davis went on board her; but did not see him.

That this Deponent thought it not prudent to be too familiar with the Prisoner, because it might tend to create a jealousy in the pirates; that the Deponent and the Prisoner (whom they suspected, because he was a forced Man) would run away together. The Deponent saith further, That Capt James Williams commander of the Ship St. Michael (whose Carpenter the Prisoner was) Intreated the said Capt Bellamy when he took him to let the Prisoner go. But the Ships company would by no means consent thereto by reason he was a Carpenter; and Swore that they would shoot him before they would let him go from them.

Capt. John Brett Mariner Sworn, saith, That he was taken by Capt. Samuel Bellamy, before the Ship Sultana was taken from Capt. Richards, and then it was the Custom among the Pirates to force no Persons, but those that remained with them were Volunteers.

Capt. Thomas Fox Sworn, saith, That he was taken by the Pirates in July last, and robbed, and they Questioned him, Whether anything was done to the Pirates in Boston Goal: The Deponent answered, He knew nothing about them. And in particular a Dutchman belonging to the Pirates, asked him about his confort a Dutch man in Boston Prison; and said, That if the Prisoners suffered they would Kill everybody they took belonging to New England.

Seth Smith Prison-keeper in Boston Sworn, saith, That when the Prisoner at the Bar was first brought to Goal, his illness hindered their talking together; but sometime after as they were discoursing, the Deponent observed to the Prisoner, That if he would be ingenuous & make a confession, he might save his Life, and be a good Evidence against the other Pirates in Prison. To which the Prisoner made answer, That he was abused by several of the Pirates that were Drowned, and was glad he had got from them, but knew nothing against the rest of the Pirates in Prison.

Then the Kings Council moved the Court that Capt. Thomas Glyn, a Prisoner for Debt upon Execution, might be brought into Court to give Evidence on His Majesty's behalf in this Trial: Whereupon the Court directed the Sheriffs, who have the keeping of His Majesty's Goal, to bring the said Glyn into Court.

Capt. Isaac Morris Sworn, saith, That on the 14th of Sept. 1716. He was taken by the Pirates, but knows nothing of Capt. Bellamy or his Accomplices.

Capt. Thomas Glyn being brought into Court by the Sheriffs, and Interrogated upon Oath, saith, That he never knew the Prisoner till he was committed to Goal for Piracy, that he frequently afterwards conversed with him, but knew nothing against him.

After which the Prisoner was desired by the President to speak for himself, Who said, That he was Carpenter of the Ship St. Michael whereof James

Williams was Capt. and Sailed out of Bristol in Great Britain in the Month of Sept. 1716. bound for Jamaica; and in Decemb. following the Ship was taken about Twenty Leagues off Sabria by two Pirate Sloops commanded by Capt Samuel Bellamy, and Monsieur Lebous, who carryed the Ships company to the Island of Blanco where they were detained till the Ninth day of January last, when he and fourteen other Prisoners were put on board the Sultan Galley, then under the said Bellamy's command who had taken her from Capt. John Richards: And afterwards took another Ship called the Whido, in which Ship to his great grief & sorrow, he was forced to come upon this Coast, where she was cast-away: And he with one John Julian only escaped Drowning He further saith, That he was no way active among the Pirates, only as he was compelled by them.

Then Mr. John Valentine the Procurator in Defence of the Prisoner observed to the Court, That if he believed the Prisoner to be guilty of the crimes, for which he was Indicted, he should not appear on his behalf: That he hoped this Honourable Court upon consideration that there was little or nothing said, much less proved against the Prisoner, they would acquit him as being Innocent, for that in all Capital crimes there must be down-right Proofs and plentiful Evidence to take away a Mans Life, and then he made the following remarks on the Evidences. Viz.

That Owen Morris Testifyed, That the Prisoner at the Bar was forced and constrained against his Will to continue with the said Capt. Bellamy and his company. And it appears by the Oath of Thomas South as well as by Morris, That the Prisoner desired Capt. Bellamy to release him upon his Caption of another Vessel according to his Promise, but his company would not consent thereto; And altho' South says, that he believes the Prisoner was on board the Scotch Vessel when her Masts were cut down, yet the Prisoner utterly denies it, and Souths belief was grounded upon hear-say.

Capt. Bretts Evidence serves only to inform the Court that the Pirates did not Press Men before the Prisoner was taken, but it is well proved, That when they took the Prisoner they compelled him to be among them, to his great sorrow and grief.

The Evidence of Thomas Glyn avails nothing, and if the Prisoner had been never so Guilty, his confession made in Prison, shall not be taken as Evidence against him on the Trial. And whereas the prisoner stands charged in the Indictment with Accumulative crimes; the Procurator in Defence was pleased to say, That in the Trial of my Lord Strafford his Attainder was reversed because he was Indicted upon Accumulative Crimes, which is contrary to Act of Parliament.

Then Oliver Noyes Esq was Sworn, and Declared, That he heard Capt. Richards say, That when he was taken by Capt. Bellamy, the Prisoner at the Bar was very desirous to be released & cryed, giving out that he was undone by being detained among them. And one of the Pirates hearing him lament his sad condition, said, Damn him, He was a Presbyterian Dog, and should fight for King James, &c.

Peter Osgood Mariner Sworn, saith, That he well knew the Prisoner, That he was a Sober, Honest Man, of good Conversation &c.

John French Sworn, saith, That he has known the Prisoner above a Year & an half being frequently with him at Bristol, and in Antegoa, that he had a good Character, and was reputed an Honest Man, &c.

Capt. John Corney Sworn, saith, That he knew the Prisoner at Antegoa, when he was Carpenter to Capt. Moor, and never heard any harm of him.

Capt. Samuel Shrimpton lately Arrived here from Jamaica, Sworn, saith, That he heard one of Davis's company say, That Davis the Prisoner was a forced Man, and he would Swear it.

Mr. Valentine moved, That an Affidavit under the firm Seal of a Notary Publick in Great Britain, and in favour of the Prisoner should be read in open Court, but his Motion was rejected, being contrary to Act of Parliament, which directs that all Evidences respecting Pirates shall be given into Court Viva Voce.

The President asked the Prisoner, What he had to say for himself: The Prisoner answered, He was not on board of the Scotch Ship that was sunk as was reported; and that he humbly conceived the Evidence produced in order to his condemnation sufficiently proved his Innocence: That his Attorney had fully spoke his Mind & Sentiments, and therefore he should not trouble this Honourable Court any longer in his Defence, or to that purpose.

THE Evidence on both sides being closed, the Advocate General reduced the whole under the following Heads. That the Indictment consisted chiefly of two parts. The first charges the Prisoner with Piracy committed by him sometime in February or March last, in the Windward passage on an English Ship named the Whido; the second with another Piracy about a Month after on a Scotch Vessel off the Capes of Virginia.

As to the first, Morris Depones, that when he was taken with Capt. Prince in the Whido he saw the Prisoner on Board the Piratical Ship Sultana, and heard Bellamy ask him, if he was willing to go, which necessarily proves that the Prisoner at that time was under no confinement, but one of the Crew, otherwise no such question could have been put to him.

This he himself acknowledges and in his Confession further declares, that tho' at first the old Pirates were a little shy of the new ones, and it seems not without good reason, they being only 80 in number to 130, yet in a short time the New Men being sworn to be faithful, and not to cheat the Company to the Value of a Piece of Eight, they all consulted and acted together with great unanimity, and no distinction was made between Old and New. Capt. Brett, who was likewise taken by Bellamy expressly says, that it was not the Pirates custom to Force any Person, and that such as were amongst them were Volunteers.

And whatever Sentiments the Prisoner might entertain of his Companions, it is plain from Capt. Fawke's Evidence that they had a very tender concern for him. Had he been really affected with so much grief and sorrow as he pretends, it was not impossible for him to have made his Escape at some of the Places where he touched before he came on this Coast, viz. Blanco, the Spanish Main, Testages and Long-Island; but it is not so much as suggested, that ever he attempted it, nor is it to be presumed as matters stood; the spoil was not yet divided, and it is obvious he expected to receive his share.

To the second, South declares, that Bellamy took the Vessel cut down her Masts and afterwards sunk her, that the Deponent being Sick at that time was told by Bellamy's Crew, and does believe, that the Prisoner went on Board the Vessel: And further saith, that the Pirates could not be prevail'd with to discharge the Prisoner because he was a Carpenter. The truth is, Bellamy sent the Prisoner and another Carpenter on Board, who by his Order cut away the Masts and bored a hole in the bottom of the Vessel, and so destroyed her. This was a piece of work properly belonging to Carpenters, and it was for performing such Services the Prisoner made himself so acceptable and necessary to his Accomplices.

To take off the weight of this Evidence it is said, that it is only Hearsay, but the Court will consider that the Deponents belief, as it is grounded on the constant Reports of 120 Persons, to whom the Fact must needs have been notoriously known, is no less certain, than if he had seen the Fact committed. But admitting the Prisoner not to be directly concerned in sinking the Vessel, yet it is clear beyond contradiction, that he was on board the Whido, and one of the Crew, that surprized and took her, and consequently Guilty of Piracy; the other Facts laid in the Indictment being only circumstances, which help to give light to the discovery of his Crimes.

For the manner of proof required in capital Crimes, especially such as are Atrocious, as in the present case, He referred the Court (in answer to what was alledged on that point in behalf of the Prisoner) to the Authorities produced already, adding, that if the Crimes did appear by the Qualifications and Circumstances as they were libelled, to be made out by undoubted presumptions, altho' every circumstance be not proved by two direct Witnesses, the same ought to be held for Clear & Plain Evidence. And as to the Exception touching Accumulative Crimes, no reply seem'd needful, it being founded on a palpable Mistake, as if Accumulative probation and Accumulative Crimes were the same.

He observed in the last place, that the only plausible Argument offered in defence of the Prisoner was his being taken and detained by Force, which he could not possibly withstand, and since Necessity has no Law, and every Man is carried on with an irresistible Ardour to any means of preserving himself, some perhaps might believe him innocent, as not being answerable for the Crimes, which for his own safety he was obliged to commit; therefore to prevent any mistake that might happen concerning this important Point, he Pray'd His Excellency and the Honourable Bench to consider,

That Force can never justify nor excuse an Action, that is contrary to the

Divine and Moral Law, for as it cannot be committed without expressing indirectly at least some contempt for the supreme Legislator, it would be the highth of impiety to think that these Laws can admit any exception of Cases of Necessity. A Man [says the very Heathen] must take care in every Moment of his Life not to recede a hairs breadth from the dictates of a good Conscience on any account whatever.

Seneca's assertion, that extream Necessity, which he calls the great protection of Humane weakness, cancels and breaks thro' every Law. is restricted only to Civil Constitutions and Establishments, and even with respect to these it is a certain and infallible rule, that altho' the doing an Action, which is prohibited may be a sure way to escape an imminent danger, yet if the evil thereby occasioned be greater or even equal to what is avoided, the Law allows no exception of necessity.

If a Man, for instance, is in danger of being kill'd or rob'd, he may lawfully in his own defence kill the aggressor, Quia versatur in re ilicita; but if to ward off the danger he should kill or rob a third person, whom he knows to be innocent, he is without doubt punishable as a Murderer or Robber. The Roman Law exempts Children and Servants acting in Obedience to their Father's and Master's command from Punishment, it being presumed they are obliged to submit, but in their perpetrating atrocious crimes, that presumption ceases and the Law considers them as free Agents . And indeed if the doctrine of Hobbes & had prevailled, i. e. that extream necessity may dispense with and supersede all Obligations Moral and Civil, there would have been no Martyrs in the Church, no examples of Loyalty in the State or honour left amongst Men. In vain did Joseph prefer a Dungeon to the imbraces of his Mistress, the Fathers of this People a far distant Wilderness to the charms of their Native Land, and the Noble Papinian death to the greatest Dignity & splendor

To conclude, The Crimes charged upon the Prisoner being direct Violations of the Laws of Nature as well as His Majesty's, and the proofs aduced being sufficient to convict him, He ought to suffer the pains of death, &c.

Where-upon the Court was cleared, and after a short debate, were of Opinion that there was good proof of the Prisoners being forced on board the Pirate Ship Whido (in which he was cast on shoar) which excused his being with the Pirates; and that there was no Evidence to prove that he was Accessory with them, but on the contrary that he was forced to stay with them against his Will. And this Question being put, Whether Thomas Davis is Guilty of Piracy, Robbery and Felony according to the Indictment, or not?

The Court Voted, That the said Thomas Davis is Not Guilty. And in less than half an Hour the Prisoner was brought again to the Bar, And the President declared, That the Court found him Not Guilty of the crimes for which he was Indicted; So he put himself on his Knees, Thanked the Court, &c. and was dismissed with a suitable Admonition. And then the Court Adjourned to Monday the Thirtieth day of December next at Nine a Clock Ante Meridiem.

Instructions to the Living, From the Condition of the Dead

This is a record of conversations Reverend Cotton Mather had with the condemned as they were led to the gallows, and a sermon he preached on the occasion.

As before, dropouts in the original manuscript are represented by diamonds and sometimes bullet points.

Instructions to the LIVING, from the Condition of the DEAD.

A Brief Relation of REMARKABLES in the Shipwreck of above One Hundred Pirates,

Who were Cast away in the Ship Whido, on the Coast of New-England, April 26. 1717.

And in the Death of Six, who after a Fair Trial at Boston, were Convicted & Condemned, Octob. 22. And Executed, Novemb. 15. 1717. With some Account of the Discourse had with them on the way to their Execution.

And a SERMON Preached their Occasion

Boston, Printed by John Allen, for Nicholas Boone, at the Sign of the Bible in Cornhill. 1717

The End of Piracy.

ANTIQUITY Entertains us with Prodigious Relations, of the Miseries which Mankind have suffered from the Growth of PIRACY. But perhaps no Example of growing. PIRACY has been more considerable, than what the

Romans were in•ested withal, after the Destruction of , and of . When those vast Cities were destroy'd, the Inhabitants not having a place of Retreat, or means of Subsistence, betook themselves to Piracy as their Profession; and there were not want People to Encourage them. 'Tis not easie to imagine the Heighth of Power, that so a Society arose unto, with which they their Dominion. All Commerce was interrupted; The City that was the Empress of the World was well nigh Starved; Some of its Magistrates as well as the other principal Citizens, fell into the Hands of the Robbers. The Coasts of Italy were everywhere molested and the Robbers with their Vessels, Entered the very Tiber, as if Rome itself were designed for a Prey unto them. The Temples and Cities, which lay near the Sea, were Sacked; and they had the Command of no less than Four Hundred Towns on the Coasts, unto which they might retire in Cases of Extremity; while other Marine Cities paid Ransomes to them for their Liberties. These Praedacious Animals, tho' they were dispersed over the whole Mediterranean, yet set up a sort of Commonwealth, and Elected Governours, and had above One Thousand Ships of several sorts, and formed Regular Fleets to carry on their Disorders. They had their Ports, their Watch-Towers, their Arsenals and Magazines; and Cilicia was, as it , their Citadel, from whence they out Supplies for their Squadrons, upon occasion. An Extraordinary Remedy was required, for a Mischief become so Formidable. The Courage and Conduct of Pompey was the Remedy. The Romans, assisted by the Rhodians, furnished Pompey, with five hundred Ships, and all the Provisions that were necessary. Pompey surpass'd the Hopes of them that Employ'd him; and in less than Three Months' time he purged the Sea of Pirates; Conquered their whole Fleet; Pursued 'em to the Fortresses they had prepared among the Rocks of Taurus; Compelled the most of them to surrender upon Discretion; and lost not one Ship in the Expedition.

Before the PIRACY on the Atlantick, by reason of whom Sailing is now dangerous, arrive to anything like what we have seen on the Mediterranean, the British Crown, Equips a Squadron of Men of War for their Extirpation. And, May our Glorious GOD success unto the Enterprize.

§ 2. In the meantime, What the Compassion of our GOD has done for

New-England, in the In··ctions of Justice on an horrid of PIRATES, which made a unto our Coast, has had in it some Occurrences, the Relation whereof may be worthy to be Preserved and Published.

About the latter end of April, there came upon the Coast Ship called, The Whido whereof one Bellamy was Commander: A Pirate Ship, of about Men, and 23 Guns. These Pirates, after many other Depraedations, took a Vessel which had Wines aboard; and put Seven of their Crew on Board, Orders to Steer after the Whido. The seven Pirates being pretty free with the Liquor, got so Drunk, that the Captive who had the Steering of the Vessel, took the opportunity of the Night, now to run her ashore, on the backside of Eastham.

A Storm was now raised and raging the Whido ignorantly following the Light of her Stranded Prize, perished in a Shipwreck, and the whole Crew were every one of them drowned, except only one Englishman, and one Indian, that were on Shore alive.

§ 3. It is ··redibly affirmed, That when these Barbarous Wretches, perceived that their Ship was breaking under them, and that they must Swim for their Lives, they horribly Murdered all their Prisoners (whereof they had a great Number) aboard; they should appear Witnesses against them. The doleful heard unto the Shore, a little before they and the Bloody Wounds found in the Bodies afterwards thrown ashore; were two great Confirmations of this Report.

How far they Wickedness of Men them.

§ 4. ...The Delivered People said, Blessed be the Lord, who hath not given us as a Prey to their Teeth!

§ 5. After some waiting for Direction, His Excellency, Colonel SHUTE, the Governour, of New-England, received, such Orders, that the Trial of the , who had not been drowned might be proceeded in.

Accordingly on Tuesday, October 22 1717. there was held at Boston, a Special Court of Admiralty (according to the Act of Parliament) for the Trial of

Simon Vanvoorst, who was Born at New-York.

John Brown, Born in Jamaica.

Thomas Baker, Born at Flushing in Holland.

Henrick Quinter, Born in Amsterdam.

Peter Cornelius Hooff, Born in Sweden.

John Shuan, Born at Nantes in France. And T. S. Born at Boston in England.

The Last was Cleared; But the other Six, after a very fair Trial, were found Guilty, and received Sentence of Death.

§ 6. The Ministers of Boston, improved the Time, which the Clemency of the GOVERNOUR allowed for that purpose, to bestow all possible Instructions upon the Condemned Criminals; Often Pray'd with them; Often Preached to them. Often Examined them and Exhorted them; and presented them with Books of Piety, suitable to their Condition. And perhaps, there is not that Place upon the face of the Earth, where more pains are taken for the Spiritual the Eternal Good of Condemned .

§ 7. On Friday, . Novemb. 15. Came o• the Execution of these Miserables. What may now be offer'd, is.

A Recollection of several Passages, which it Discourse with the Prisoners while they walked from the Prisoner to the Place of Execution.

I. Minister.

Your determined Hour…Cry in the Destruction which GOD this Afternoon brings upon you. I am come to help you what I can, that your Cry may turn to some Good Account. How do you find your Heart now disposed?

Baker.

Oh! I am a dreadful Condition! Lord JESUS, Dear JESUS, Look upon me!

Min.

You are sensible, That you have been a very Great Sinner and that you are by your Sins Exposed unto the dreadful Displeasure of the Glorious and Holy GOD;—Hands, which it is a fearful Thing to fall into!

Baker.

Oh! Yes; I am! And is it possible that such a Sinner should ever find mercy with GOD! O GOD, wilt thou pardon such a Sinner!

Min.

My Friend, This is the very First Thing that I am to advise you of. There is a Pardon to be had! The Blessed GOD has made this Gracious Proclamation; That His Name is, A GOD Gracious and Merciful, Forgiving Iniquity, and

Transgression and Sin. He is a GOD Ready to pardon. 'Tis your Duty to Lay hold on the Proclamation. The Pardoning Mercy of GOD is an Infinite Mercy. You have not Sinned beyond the Bounds of a Mercy that has no Bounds. Poor man, Try to Believe, Embrace, Admire this Wonderful Mercy. You have Sinned enough already: Don't add the Sin of Despair to all the rest. Our Good GOD is One who takes pleasure in them that hope in His Mercy.

Baker.

Oh! I wish I could! I wish I could!

Min.

GOD help thee! I say this to you, As Great as your Sins have been, there are now Comforted in the Paradise of GOD, the Spirits of some who once committed the very same that you are now guilty of.

Baker.

Lord! I have been guilty of all the Sins in the World!

Min.

But now, O Give all the Attention of a Dying man I am to shew you, how the Pardening Mercy of GOD may come to reach ...Died for as; has undergone the that is due to as for our Sins has had His Blood shed as for us. This Blood obtains a full for all that come and humbly plead with the Dispositions of ...

Baker.

1 paragraph

Min.

1 paragraph

...may dy such a Death as my Saviour died! Oh! that my Mind may be filled with the Love of God, and have the Image of my SAVIOUR produced in it. These Wishes will flame in you wonderfully, if the Blood of your SAVIOUR be Sprinkled on you, for a Pardon.

Baker.

Oh! I can't come I can do nothing Pity me, O GOD! Sweet JESUS, Pity me!

Min.

I'll mention to you a sweet word of your Great SAVIOUR; A word worth a Thousand Worlds! Have you not a mighty Load Lying on you?

Baker.

Oh! A Load, A Load that is the heavy for me.
Min.
Now heat the Word of your SAVIOUR: Come to me, All ye that Labour, and are heavy & I will give you Rest. Answer it; But first Look to Him, for to give the Answer; O my SAVIOUR I come unto thee!
Baker.
O Almighty GOD. Look upon me.
Min.
 perceive you are : very Great But must be with such at
II. Min.
Poor Vanvoorst, What shall done for thee? How do you find your Heart, in the dreadful Hour, that is now come upon you!
Vanvoorst.
I hope, a Little than it has been.
Min.
You will give all possible Attention, unto the Admonition of Piety, which are now to be given you.

Tho' you have so wickedly Chosen Other Gods; Yet the Glorious GOD, is Willing to be Your GOD. The GOD, have denyed so many thousands of times; the GOD whose Baptism you have Sinned against the GOD against whom you have Rebelled, after you had been by Religious Parents dedicated unto Him; This GOD is yet Willing to be Your GOD. And if you have Him for Your GOD; then you are Happy to all Eternity! You will have a Place in His Holy City assign'd unto you.
V. V.
What shall I do to be so Happy?
Min.
Nothing in your own Strength. But having begg'd of GOD, that He would Strengthen you. You must first Bewail it Bitterly, that you have Served Other Gods. You have set up your Self in the Throne of GOD. You have placed on the Riches of this World, the Dependence you should have, had only on GOD. You have hearkened unto Satan more than unto GOD. Are you Sorry for this?
V. V.

I hope, I am.

Min.

Well; What remains is this. Our Great SAVIOUR is the Head of His People in the Covenant of GOD. You come into the Covenant of GOD, and He becomes Your GOD, when you heartily Consent, that your SAVIOUR do for you those two Grand Things which in His Covenant with GOD for His People, He Engaged the doing of. GOD help you to understand this important Matter. Attend unto the Two Proposals.

In the first place, Do you Consent unto this; That the Sacrifice of your Great SAVIOUR, should be your Atonement; and that GOD should be favourable to you for the sake of that alone?

V. V.

I hope I do.

Min.

But then, at the same time, Do you heartily Consent unto this; That your SAVIOUR should by His Good spirit quicken you to Live unto GOD; and render every Sin Loathsome unto you; and incline you to everything that is Holy and Just and Good; and give you a New Heart; and make you a New Creature; and set up His Kingdom in your Soul, and Dwell and Rule there forever.

V. V.

I hope I do.

Min.

In thus Returning to GOD, it is most necessary, that you should have in Heart full of Contrition, from the Sense of your horrid Sins against Him.

V. V.

I have been very Great Sinner.

Min.

Of all your past Sins, which are they, that now by most heavy upon you?

V. V.

My Undutifulness unto my Parents; And my Profanation of the Sabbath.

Min.

Your Sinning against a Religious Education, is a fearful Aggravation of all your Sins. I pray you, to count it so.

V. V.

I do, Sir.

Min.

But I wish, that you, and all your miserable Companions here, were more sensible of the Crime, for which you are presently to be chased from among the Living.

Robbery, and Piracy! You felt the Light of GOD in your own Soul, condemning you for it, while you were committing of it. All Nations agree, to treat your Tribe, as the Common Enemies of Mankind, and Extirpate them out of the World. Besides all this, and the Miseries you brought on many good people, in their Disappointed Voyages, I am told, that some were Kill'd in your subduing of them. You are Murderers! Their Blood cries to Heaven against you. And so does the Blood of the poor Captives; [Fourscore, I hear,] that were drown'd, when the Whidaw was Lost in the Storm, which cast you on Shore

V. V.

We were Forced Men.

Min.

Forced! No; There is no man who can say, He is Forced unto any Sin against the Glorious GOD! Forced! No; You had better have Suffered anything, than to Sinn'd as you have done. Better have died a Martyr by the cruel Hands of your Brethren, than have become one of their Brethren.

Or, If I should allow that you were at first a Forced Man, what were you, when you came upon the Coast of Cape-Cod? Were not you one of those, who came Aboard the Prize, wherein you were Lost? When the Ma•e so managed the Tack, that you Lost the Sight of the Whidau, and you might have Escaped easily from your Masters into our Arms, did not you Ca•se the Mate, and Compel him with a thousand Menaces, to Recover the Sight of your Sh•p? After your Shipwreck, did you fly into our Arms like men Escaped of Prison? Or, did not you Endeavour still such a Flight from us, as Enable you Return unto the Trade you were now used •nto? Is this the Conduct of a Forced Man?

We are Blessed with one of the Best GOVERNOURS a Person of uncommon Goodness, and Candour, and Clemency. He was is full of Desire to have shown Mercy, unto you and your Friend Baker here, as was possible. Instances were made unto him on your behalf, by Friends; whom he set all possible value upon: I myself bore my part in the pressing. Instances. But, when he Remonstrated unto us, the strong and full Proofs which there were of your being Active Pirates; and of your having the Cry of so much Innocent Blood against you; and we saw, his Apprehension, that he could not answer it unto GOD, no more than unto the King, (whose Commands for all Severity upon you were very positive) we could say no more; but must Approve and Applaud the Inflexible Justice that we see joined with a Temper full of Mercy in him.

Say now; What think you of the Bad Life, wherein you have Wandred from God? Can you say nothing, that your Worthy Parents, (whom you have so kill'd!.) may take a little Comfort from! have some Light in their Darkness?

V. V.

I am heartily sorry for my very bad Life. I dy with hope that GOD Almighty will be Merciful to me. And I had rather Dy this Afternoon, I would Chuse Death, rather than return to such a Life as I have Lived; rather than Repeat my Crimes.

Min.

'Tis a Good and a Great Speech; But such as I have heard uttered by some, who after a Reprieve, (which you cannot have) have returned unto their Crimes. I must, now Leave you, in the Hands of Him who Searches the Heart; and beg of Him, Oh! May there be such an Heart in you!

III. Min.

Brown, In what State, in what Frame, does thy Death, now within a few Minutes of thee, find thee.

Brown.

Very Bad! Very Bad!

Min.

You see yourself then a most miserable Sinner.

Br.

Oh! most Miserable!

Min.

You have had an Heart Wonderfully bardened.

Br.

Ay, and it grows harder. I don't know what is the matter with me. I can't but wonder at myself!

Min.

There is no Help to be had, anywhere, but in the admirable SAVIOUR, whom I am now to point you to. Behold, an Admirable SAVIOUR so calling on you, Look to me and be Saved. O Wonderful Call! Salvation to be had for a Look!

Br.

Ay, But I can't Look!

Min.

Ah, poor, sad, lost Creature, Look for Help to Look! But mind, What I say unto you. Set your Heart unto these Things, They are your Life it. You are to Look unto your SAVIOUR, in all his Offices, for all His Benefits, you would hope to be received by a SAVIOUR, who Receiveth Sinners.

First, You must Consider your SAVIOUR, as a Priest; and you must say to Him, O my SAVIOUR, I Rely upon thy Blood, that I may be cleansed from all my Sin! Is this the Language of your Soul?

Br.

Yes, Syr.

Min.

You must Consider your SAVIOUR then also as your Prophet; and you must say unto Him; O my SAVIOUR, Teach me thy Ways; and let not a Deceived Heart be my Ruine at the last! Is this also the Language of your Soul?

Br.

Yes, Syr.

Min.

You must now Consider your SAVIOUR as your King; and you must say unto Him; O my SAVIOUR, Enter into my Heart . Set up thy Throne there; Let thy Law be written there. all the Enmity of my Carnal Mind against

GOD. Cause me to Love Him! I• this the Language of your Soul?

Br.

Yes, Syr.

Min.

Oh! I wish it may be so. I take notice, you have your Prayer Book with Forms of Prayer, may of use to those who need the Assistances. You have had such put into your Hands; and you have also had the Bible bestow'd on you, with Leafs folded unto Psalms, proper for you to turn into Prayers. But after all. A Soul touched with a sense of your Condition, and fired with the Sight of what and what you want, and what our SAVIOUR is willing to do for you, will cause you to Pray, beyond that any Forms in the World can do. I am jealous, that what you read sometimes, is rather for an Amusement, than from any real and lively Sentiment raised in you: For some of the Prayers you Read, are not pertinent unto your Condition. Friend, Make that Prayer, O Lord, I beseech then, deliver my Soul! Make that Prayer, O Lord, Gather not my Soul with Sinners! Make that Prayer, God be merciful to me a . These are Great Prayers, though ones Great Prayers, when they proceed from an Heartbroken before the Lord.

Br.

Oh! God be merciful to me Sinner!

Min.

A Sinner. Alas, What cause to say so! But, I pray• What more Special Sins, Ly now as a more heavy Burden on you?

Br.

Special Sins! Why, I have been guilty of all the Sins in the World! I know not where to begin. I may begin with Gaming! No, Whoring, That Led on to Gaming; and Gaming Led on to Drinking; and Drinking to Lying, and Swearing, and Cursing, & all that is bad; and so to Thieving; And so to This!

Min.

You ought now to Dy Warning of all People, against these Paths of the Destroyer.

I will say to you, but this one thing more. GOD has distinguished you from your Drowned Brethren, by giving you a Space to Repent, which was denied unto them. I am Sorry you have made no Better use of it. It may be, the Space has been given, because GOD may have some of His Chosen, among the Six Children of Death. GOD forbid, that the Space must be of no use to you, but only to aggravate you Condemnation, when you appear before Him.

IV. Min.

Hoof; A melted Heart would now'be a comfortable Symptom upon thee. Do you find anything of it.

Hoof.

Something of it; I wish it were more!

Min.

To pursue this Good Intention, I will now give a Blow with an Hammer, that breaks the Rocks to pieces. I will bring you the most Heart-melting Word, as ever was heard in the World. We find in the Sacred Scripture such a word as this; CHRIST, who is GOD, does beseech you, Be ye Reconciled unto GOD. That ever the Son of GOD, should come to us, with such a Message from His Eternal Father! What? After we have so Offended His Infinite Majesty! After we have been so Vile, so Vile!—and He stands in so little Need of us!—To beseech such Criminals, to be Reconciled unto the Holy GOD, and be willing to be Happy in His Favour. O Wonderful! Wonderful! Methinks, it cannot be heard without flowing Tears of Joy!

Ho.

Ah! But what shall I'do to be Reconciled unto GOD!

Min.

Make an Answer, make an Echo, unto this Wonderful Word of your SAVIOUR. And, what can you make but this?—And for this also, you must have the Help of His Grace to make it; O my dear SAVIOUR, I beseech thee to Reconcile me unto GOD.

Ho.

Oh! That it might be so!

Min.

A Reconciliation to GOD it the Only thing that you have now to be concern'd about. If this be not accomplished, before a few minutes more are Expired, you go into the Strange Punishment reserved for the Workers of

Iniquity. You go, where He that made you, will not have Mercy on you; He that formed you, will shew you no favour. But it is not yet altogether Too Late. An Hearty Consent the Motions of the , will prepare you to pass from an Ignominious Death, into an Inconceivable Glory.

Ho.

Oh! Let me hear them!

Min.

First, You must Consent unto This; O, my SAVIOUR, I fly to thy Sacrifice; I beg, I beg, that for the sake of That, thy Wrath may be turned away from me; I cannot bear to have thy Wrath Lying on me! Can you say so!

Ho.

I say it, I say it!

Min.

But then, You must Consent unto This also; O my SAVIOUR, I Cry unto thee, to take away all that is contrary to GOD in my Soul; and cause me to Love GOD with all my Soul; and Conquer my depraved Will; and bring to Rights all that is Wrong in my Affections; and let my Will become entirely subject unto the Will of GOD in all things. Can you say so.

Ho.

I say it, I say it!

Min.

If it be heartily said, The Reconciliation is accomplished. But if you were to Live your Life over again, how would you live it?

Ho.

Not as I have done!

Min.

How then?

Ho.

In Serving of GOD, and in doing of Good unto Men.

Min.

GOD Accept you. Oh! That your SAVIOUR, might now say to you, as He said in a Dying Hour, unto One, who died as a Thief, This Day thou shalt be with me in Paradise. I do with some Encouragement leave you in His

Glorious Hands.

Ho.

O my dear JESUS! I Lay hold on thee; and I resolve, never, never, to let thee go!

Min.

May He help you to keep your Hold, of the Hope set before you.

Ho.

My Death this Afternoon, 'tis nothing, 'tis nothing; Tis the wrath of a terrible GOD after Death abiding on me, which is all that I am afraid of.

Min.

There is a JESUS, who delivers from the Wrath to come; With Him I Leave you.

V. Min.

Quinter, Thou art come into a Dark Time.

Quinter.

'Tis a Dark Time with me.

Min.

But will you receive it, if I bring you Light in this Darkness!

Q.

God be merciful to me!

Min.

One who had been a Great Sinner, had this Experiment, I said, I confess my Transgressions unto the thou forgavest the Iniquity of May not this be your Experience too!

Qu.

I wish it may!

Min.

When you have Sinned, you have swallowed a Deadly Poyson. With a of Repentance, and Confession, you must cast up this Deadly If your Soul go away with it, you are Banished from GOD, and fixed in Eternal Miseries.

Qu.

What shall I do?

Min.

Do you Confess, That you are a very Great Sinner

Qu.

Yes, I confess, I have committed all manner of Sins.

Min.

Are you Sorry for what you have done?

Qu.

Heartily Troubled.

Min.

But are you sensible, That you have an Heart full of Sin; An Heart that is desperately wicked? All the Sin in your Life, came out of your Heart. Are you Troubled, that you have such an Heart?

Qu.

Heartily Troubled.

Min.

Look up to GOD for New Heart?

Qu.

With all my Heart.

Min.

Do you own that GOD is Righteous in all the Evil that is some upon you?

Qu.

Yes, I do.

Min.

But now, Your Confession must be made, with a Faith Leaning on the Great Sacrifice. On every Stroke in your Confession of your Sin, must add; Lord, Pardon my Sin, for the sake of the Blood of my SAVIOUR.

Qu.

I desire to do so.

Min.

But, we are taught, He that confess•t• and forsaketh shall find mercy. You will have no Opportunity now, for the Experiment of a Reformed Life; You cannot now Live to see, whether you don't Return unto Folly. But however, your Heart must be so set against all Sin, that your Choice must be, Rather to Dy than to Sin.

Tho' cannot show you Mercy; your is forfeited, beyond the Reach of Mercy from the Government; yet upon a True Repentance, you will find Mercy with GOD. Repentance is also Gift. Oh! Keep Looking up unto Him; Lord, Give me a Repenting Heart! O my SAVIOUR, Thou givest Repentance and Remission of Sins!

Man, Thy Immortal SOUL is presently to Return unto GOD. A SOUL doing so, can look for nothing but His Fiery Indignation, and a dreadful Banishment from Him; Except it be a SOUL with another Biass upon it, than what men have in their Depraved Nature. It must be, A SOUL to which a CHRIST is Precious; to which a CHRIST is the Prince of Life, the Living Spring of all that is Good: A SOUL to which all Sin is odious, and more Bitter than Death: A SOUL groaning under all its Evil Inclinations, as the most heavy Burdens; A SOUL sick of attemts to find Satisfaction in Creatures: A SOUL desirous above all things to Serve and please the Glorious GOD.

My Friend, May thy SOUL now be found so disposed!

VI. The Last among the Sons of Death, was a poor Frenchman, (called John Shuan,) to whom, inasmuch as he understood not English, and had been a Roman Catholick, the Minister thus applied himself.

Min.

O Pecheur tres-miserable. Vous estes un Prisonnier• de la Justice; Mais Vous estes un Prisonnier de L' Esperance.

Notre Seigneur et Sauveur JESUS CHRIST, est L' Esperance des Pecheurs; Et il ny a point de Salut en aucun autre.

Cette parole est Certaine, et digne d'etre Entierement receue; C'est que JESUS CHRIST est venu au monde, pour Souver les pecheurs.

Mais il est fort necessaire, d'invequer votre Sauveur.

Vous pleurez d'une maniere Lamentable; Las! Miserable Ie suis; qui me delivra?

JESUS CHRIST Le Grand Sauveur du Monde, respond, Regardez vors s•yez Sauvez. Entendez vous•

Shuan.

Ouy, Monsieur. Ie l'entende bien.

Min.

Ah, Mon Frere! Les Cordeaux de la Mart vous avoient Environnez; Et Les destresses d'Enfer vous avoient rencontrez. Mais, Invoquez Le Nom de l'Eternel, disant, Ie te prie, Eternel, Delivre mon Ame.

O meschant, Retourntz a L'eternel, et it pitie do vous, et il pardonnera or plus.

Entenaez vous?

Shuan.

Ouys Monsieur; le vous remercy.

Min.

Mais it faut que vous vous contentions du seul Sacrifice, et de L'Intercession de JESUS CHRIST. pardon de ses pechez, par sa propres merites, ou par la Mediation de quelqua Creature. faut, que votre priere soit, L'Obeissance de JESUS CHRIST a ta Loy, O mon Dieu, est Se•le Justice. En Consideration de catte se•le Justice, fai que l' obtienne pardon et Favenr •upres de Tol. le Renonce, le Renonce, a tous autres Mediatours.

Que dites vous! Renoncez vous tous Mediateurs!

Shuan.

Ie ne scay pas ce que le diray.

le remets votre Esprit en la votre Redempteur JESUS CHRIST.

Translated into English, at the Desire of the Bookseller.

'Min.

Most Miserable Sinner; You are a Prisoner of Justice, but, you are yet a Prisoner of Hope.

One Lord and Saviour JESUS CHRIST is the Hope of Sinners; and indeed there is not Salvation in any other.

This is a Saving most certain, and worthy to be of all Entirely received; That JESUS CHRIST is Come into the World, for to save Sinners.

But it is most Necessary, that you call upon your Saviour.

You make this Lamentable Outcry, O wretched man that I am; who shall deliver me!

JESUS CHRIST, the Great SAVIOUR of the World, gives this Answer, Look unto me, and be Saved.

Understand you what I say?

Shuan.

Yes, Syr; I understand you very well.

Min.

Ah, My Brother; The Cords of Death compass you, the Anguishes of Hell come upon you. But now, Call on the Name of the LORD, and say, O Lord, I beseech thee, Deliver my Soul.

Sinful Man, Return to the Lord, and He will have pity on you; and He will abundantly pardon you.

Do you understand me?

Shuan.

Yes Syr; and I thank you.

Min.

But you must then take up with the Only Sacrifice and Intercession of JESUS CHRIST. No one comes at the Pardon of his Sins, on the account of his own Deserts, or thro' the Mediation of any Creature. Your Prayer must be this, O my GOD, The Obedience of JESUS CHRIST unto thy Law is my only Righteousness For the sake of that Righteousness only grant that I may find pardon and mercy with thee! I Renounce, I Renounce all other Mediators.

What do you say to This? Do you Renounce all other Mediators?

Shuan.

I can't well tell, what to say to it?

Min.

I commit your Spirit into the Hand of JESUS CHRIST, your Redeemer.

At the Place of Execution, a Prayer was made by a Minister of the City; The Chief Heads whereof were;

An Adoration of the Divine Justice in the Evil pursuing Sinners;—

—Whereof here was now a dismal Spectacle;—

—And of the Divine Mercy in the Forgiveness offered unto Chief of Sinners.

A Confession of what we have Committed, when we have Sinned;

—And of what we have Deserved;

—And of the Wicked Heart, which does Expose to all.

An Admiration of the Grace, which is Ready to Pardon;

And of the Blood which does purchase the Pardon;

With an Essay to Lay hold on it.

And Aspirations after the Token and Effect of a Pardon, in an Heart hating of, and mourning for, all Sin, and filled with the Love of GOD.

An Application of these things more particularly unto the Case of the Miserables now standing on the Scaffold;—

With ardent Cries to Heaven, that Free Grace might yet have Triumphs and Wonders in them; and all Heaven be filled with Praises.

—Pleading, That nothing Less than an Almighty Arm, could change such Vicious and Obstinate Hearts as theirs; but that the Holy Spirit, who is the Arm of the LORD, is nothing Less than the Almighty GOD.

A Supplication, that GOD would Sanctifie the horrible Spectacle unto the vast Croud of Spectators now assembled; and Effectually Caution them to Shun the Paths of the Destroyer.

Especially, the Young People; That they might Betimes give themselves up to the Conduct of their SAVIOUR; Left their Disobedience provoke Him, to Leave them in the Hands of the Destroyer.

And a Supplication for our Sea-faring People; That they may more generally Turn and Live unto GOD; That they may not fall into the Hands of Pirates; That such as are fallen into their Hands, may not fall into their Wayes; That the poor Captives may with Cries to GOD that shall pierce the Heavens, procure His Good Providence to work for their Deliverance; And, That the Pirates now infesting the Seas, may have a Remarkable Blast from Heaven following of them; the Sea-monsters, of all the most cruel, be Extinguished; and that the Methods now taking by the British Crown for the Suppression of these Mischiefs may be prospered.

On the Scaffold, as the Last Minute came on, several of the Malefactors, discovered a great Consternation.

Baker and Hoof appeared very distinguishingly Paenitent.

But Brown, behaved himself at such a rate, as one would hardly imagine that any Compos Mentis, could have done so. He broke out into furious Expressions, which had in them too much of the Language he had been used unto. Then he fell to Reading of Prayers, not very pertinently chosen. At length he made a Short Speech, which everybody trembled at; Advising

Sailors, to beware of all wicked Living, such as his own had been; especially to beware of falling into the Hands of the Pirates: But if they did, and were forced to join with them, then, to have a care whom they kept, and whom they let go, and what Countries they come into.

In such amazing Terms did he make his Exit! With such Madness, Go to the Dead!

The rest said Little, only Vanvoorst, having (with Baker) Sung a Dutch Psalm, Exhorted Young. Persons to Lead a Life of Religion, and keep the Sabbath, and carry it well to their Parents.

Behold, Reader, The End of Piracy!

Warnings to Them that make Haste to be Rich

A sermon preached by Reverend Cotton Mather on the day of the pirate's execution

BOSTON. 27. d. VIII. m. 1717.
JER. XVII. 2.
He that getteth Riches and not by Right, shall leave them in the midst of his Days, and at his End shall be a Fool.

a very sad , a very black Tragedy, which entertains us, in a just Sentence of DEATH passed upon a Great Number of PIRATES, who have made their wicked Attempts to and not by Right, and are now leave them, and all the World, in the midst of their Days; Their End, and a fearful End is come; in which their Folly is with the most insupportable Stings now charged upon them. What are these PIRATES now, but so many Preachers of those Things; which once they could not bear to hear the Servants of GOD Preach unto them? Unhappy, but Practical, and Oh! why not Powerful, Preachers of the Evil which pursueth Sinners, and of the Destruction and Misery found in the Ways of Ungodliness and of Dishonesty. It will be our Folly, if the Voice of such Warners be not understood, pondered, hearken'd to; 'Twill be a proper Exercise of Wisdom, in the Winners of Souls, to make the Voice of their Warnings as Articulate and Effectual, as 'tis possible. My Heare••, The Condition of these wretched Men, is to Preach unto you; and I now read their Text unto you; A Text on which they give you a very dismal Commentary.

The Sinful People, on whom by his Prophets denounced very destroying Judgments for their Sins, were yet very confident of their escaping the Destruction threatend unto them. One Ground of their Carnal Confidence was this; They were a Wealthy People; And they were an Instance of a Proverb, which one of their own Kings had left with them; The Rich Mans Wealth is his City, and as an high Wall in his own conceit. My Text pulls down the High Wall of their Strong City, and shows them the Folly of their vain Imaginations. They were a Rich People, 'tis true; But then, what Riches they had, they did not come honestly by them. They got Riches, but not by Right. Their Great Persons had generally got their Great Estates in Ways forbidden by GOD, Ways offensive to GOD: Now it could not be well expected, that such, or their Estates could be things. No; As the Woodcock on what it did not lay, so is he that Riches and not by Right. But Rapacious Bird, What becomes of it? Shall it long enjoy the Nest which it hath so praedatiously siez'd upon? By no means: He shall leave them in the midst of his Days, and at his End he shall be a Fool. Convinced of his own Folly, he shall call himself, A Fool; and all the World from the Conviction of what they see, shall also agree to call him so.

My DOCTRINE, will be a Voice of the LORD, from Occurrents which we see upon the Waters, and you hear the God of Glory Thundring in it.

RICHES not gotten Honesty are gotten Foolishly; and the dreadful Death which comes at the End of an Unjust Life, will terribly proclaim the Folly of it.

The Peals of Thunders are to be distinctly heard in the PROPOSITIONS.

I. It is no rare thing, I am sorry say so!—that Riches are got, or sought, but not so Honestly as they ought to be. 'Tis often so, that Men would get Riches, but not by Right.

But who are these Workers of Iniquity? The Hue-in-cry after the Men who are to be Indicted for the Crimes of Trespassing upon the Rules of Honesty in the pursuit of Riches; 'tis to be taken out of the Eighth Commandment. The Trespasses of Men on what is implied in the Eighth Commandment, and all Essays unjustly to sieze, or keep, what belongs unto another; These are the Points wherein Men go to get Riches and not by Right.

But I shall single out some, that are more Notorious Transgressors in the Ways of Dishonesty; and assure them, that they belong to the Tribe of Evil-doers.

sure, the PIRATE at Sea, and the Robber on Shore, is one who to get Riches and not by Right. here it may be complained, That the Laws reach the lesser Pirates Robbers, there are, as one of them too truly told the Execrable Alexander, much Greater Ones, whom no Humane Laws presume to meddle withal: Monsters, whom we dignify with the Title of Hero's: Conquerors and Emperors, but yet no other than a more splendid sort of Highway-man. Of these, Many have done abominably; But thou, the Leviathan lately at Versailles, hast excelled them all.

But it must also be asserted, That he who loves to Oppress, or to Extort from another, what he has no Legal Claim unto, the same is Brother to a Thief. When 'tis become Necessary for a Man to have such or such a Commodity, and his Neighbour takes advantage of his Necessity, to scrue unreasonably upon him; When a Man takes advantage from his Neighbours being Low, and Mean, and Weak, and compells him to Hard Bargains him; then he goes to get Riches not by Right. He who would escaped the Devouring Fire, and Everlasting Burnings, must be one who despises the Gain of such Oppressions.

But then, he who Pilsers from his Neighbour, or privately takes any of his Possessions from him, without some Allowance from him for it; This is the proper Thief: All the World Brands him for such an one. What he gets, is most unquestionably not by Right. Neighbours must be some Way Agreed about it, before one may take what belongs unto another.

All Fraud in Dealing, must also be condemned as a sort of Theft. Cheating and Lying, in Dealing, is but Stealing. To warrant a thing for Sound, and Good, and so and so Valuable, when it may be known to be otherwise; To draw a thing out of anothers hands by any False Talk about the matter; To use False Weights, and False Scales, and False Measures

This may be to get Riches; but it is by Right; You cannot think it is!

Men may get Riches also, but you be sure, 'tis not by Right, When 'tis a Trade of Sin which they make their Earnings of: If they get Money by the direct advancing of Idolatry; By Fortune-telling; By Unchastity; By playing the Pimp, or Band; Or, By serving the Lusts, which ought to be mortifyed.

Gaining by Gaming is as bad. It is to get the Estate of a Neighbour at a Price, which it ought not to be staked at. If he be such a Sot, as to stake anything of his Estate at such a Price, our Charity should not permit us to take it from him. Surely, O Man, Thou durst not pray over this way of getting, and seriously and solemnly Beg of the Glorious GOD, O Lord, I beseech thee, send now Prosperity! A Clear Proof, 'Tis not by Right!

And, I pray, Why should the setting up of Lotteries, be esteemed a Christian and a Credible Way of Living? Methinks, No Man that Examine them, can Justify them .

The Men also, that run rash Debt, and care not how much, how long they ly in Debt; and will Borrow, without any View, or Care of Paying again: I would ask of the Creditors, Thinkest thou this to be Right.

I will declare one thing more unto you; Not only Unfaithful Treasurers, but also, Judges, who take Bribes, either to pass a wrong Judgment, or •••passing a Right one: Lawyers who take Fees, for pleading a Case, which they know to be an Ill one; Rulers, who Sell the publick Places of Trust, to which Merit should be the only Recommendation: These too, may get Riches: But when the World that groans under it, shall be delivered from the Bondage of Corruptions, what they do will be condemned, as Not by Right. You may Flatter your selves, in your own Eyes, O ye Greedy Ones, As doing only what is Customary: But your Iniquity will be found hateful, and it will be found a Filthy Lucre, that you are Greedy of.

 Stroke more, shall finish my of The Methods wherein Men get Riches and not by Right; It is done, when Men withhold more than is meet, and allow not a due Portion of their Estates unto Pious Uses. A Fault, which provokes the Holy One to withhold His Blessing from them. They fancy, they get Riches by this Parsimony; but it eventually tends unto Poverty!

These People, all pray the Fool.

But this is what I am going more fully to advertise you of.

II. The Men who seek to get Riches, but not Honestly, they do very Foolishly. The Man who gets Riches, and not by Right, will most certainly be found a

Fool at the last. We shall all presently see the Exaltation of this Folly.

First. Most Certainly, Sin is Folly. How often, how often, has the Wisdom of GOD, in his Holy Oracles, call'd it so? No Man ever Sins, but he transgresses the Rules of Wisdom It may be said of him, as in Prov. V. 23. In the Greatness of his Folly he goes astray. And his Confession must be that, 2 Sam. XXIV. 10.

I have sinned in what I have done, and I have done very foolishly.

Now when Riches are not got Honestly, they are got Sinfully. If they are not got by Right, they are got by Sin. The Law of the Glorious God is, Thou shalt not Covet. But there is an Evil Coveteousness in them, who get Riches, and not by Right. The Law of the Glorious GOD is, All things that you would have men do to you, do ye even so to them. They who get Riches, and not by Right, are those, who do not as they would be done unto. The Law of the Glorious GOD is, That no man over-reach, or defraud his Brother in any matter. They who get Riches, and not by Right, are such as Over-reach and Defraud their Brethren. Yea, O Man, What doth the Lord require of thee, but to do justly? Such Laws of the Only wise God, cannot without the most insolent Folly be trampled on.

But Secondly; If Men will get Riches and not by Right, Let us enquire, Whether they don't lose more than they get. If they do so, 'tis most evidently an Egregious Folly which they are guilty of. Now, O Man, by unjust Gain, encreasing thy Substance, Come and see me state thy Accompts, and from thy most certain Losses, learn how foolishly thy Business has been carryed on.

First; It is an astonishing Truth, and among them that walk in the Ways of Dishonesty, it falls down like a flaming Thunderbolt!—Foolish Men, All the Riches which are not Honestly gotten, must be lost in a Shipwreck of Honest Restitution, if ever Men come unto Repentance and Salvation. There is no Man, who gets Riches and not by Right, but the Repentance, unto Salvation, will bring him to that Language Zacheus; LUK. XIX. 8.

Lord, I Restore. My Friends, 'Tis a tremendous Lesson of Christianity, which I am now treating you withal. Oh! tremble before it. It is, RESTITUTION, RESTITUTION; without which all things not Honestly gotten, will remain and corrode, as an Eternal Poison in the Soul of the Offender. If you get Riches and not by Right, it must be Repented of; it must be Repented of: A Righteous God who loveth Righteousness, will banish you out of His Kingdom, if it be not Repented of. Now, there can be nothing plainer than this; That if you Retain in your hands, what you have gotten and not by Right, you do not Repent of what you have done. You cannot Repent, if you do not Refund unto the utmost of your Capacity. Of a Man who has got Riches and not by Right, we are told Job XX. 15.

He hath swallowed down Riches, and he shall vomit them up again, GOD shall cast them out of his Belly. O Unjust Man, look for a terrible Vomit. Either God will by Scourges, make thee throw up thy Unjust Gain, and fetch it out of thee by one Impoverishing Stroke after another; Or else, He will by Repentance dispose thee, to throw it up, with an active, equal, patient Restitution. Alas, what hast thou been a doing? A Restitution of all thy Ill-gotten Treasures must be endeavoured, if thou wouldest not shut thy self out from the Everlasting Mercies of GOD. Ah! How fearfully, how fatally, how irrecoverably are the Souls of many Unjust Men entangled in the Snares of Death? They cannot hope to find Favour with GOD, or an Acceptance among true Paenitents, if they do not endeavour all the Restitution that is possible. But will they ever come to this? No, The Vomit is too strong for them; they'll sooner dye than come unto it! Foolish Men; You have at once lost all that you have got! You must with your own hands throw all over-board, if you would not be drown'd in Perdition at the Last!

Secondly. A Good Esteem is lost, by them who get Riches in the Ways of Dishonesty; A Good Esteem among all those, who are willing to live in all Godliness and Honesty. We have been told, Prov. XXII. 1.

A good Name is rather to be chosen than great Riches. 'Tis far more Honourable and Reputable, to be a Good Man, than to be a Rich Man. It will most of all be found so, in the Day when every Man shall receive Praise of God, who is found worthy of it. But now as a Thief is ashamed when he is found, so 'tis a shameful Thing to be found a False-dealer in any Degree, in any Affair: It makes a Man lightly esteemed. All Baseness in any Dealing, is a Blemish on the Dealer. To Deal unjustly with any Man; 'tis a Blot in any

Scutcheon. The Kings themselves that have done it, are of, of what Memory, I beseech you? No one believes it, if they say, A Blessed One.

Thirdly, Yea, a Good Conscience is Lost. And that's a worse Loss, a Thousand Times; a Loss which if we were wise, we should at any time take Joyfully the Spoiling of our Goods, for the preventing of! When a man gets Riches and not by Right, he has a Conscience within him, which tells him, He does what he ought not to do. The Servant of GOD could say; Heb. XIII. 18.

We have a Good Conscience, in all things willing to Live honestly. Men don't keep a Good Conscience, when they don't Live Honestly. The man that has taken more than his own, is he, of whom we read, A Dreadful Sound is in his Ears; And again, Terrors shall make him afraid on every side. His Wounded Conscience keeps roaring in his Ears; Thou hast wronged thy Neighbour, and there is a Just GOD, who is a dreadful Revenger of such Wrongs at these. 'Tis a Folly for a man to in•ur the Reproaches of an Angry Conscience.

All the Riches of a Chaldean or Persian Monarch, would be too dearly bought, if a man must have them accompanied with the Lashes of a Guilty Conscience, furiously Reproaching of him. All the Relish of Riches is Lost; Rocks of Diamonds, & Mountains of Gold, are not worth a Straw; where the Conscience is like the Troubled Sea, and there is no peace unto the Wicked!

Fourthly; The Loss of the SOUL is horribly Endangered; Yea, without Repentance, the Danger is Unavoidable. And oh! that the awful words of our SAVIOUR, who knew the Worth of a SOUL, were duly considered with us; Mat. XVI. 26.

What is a man profited, if he gain the whole World, and Lose his own Soul! We commonly say, One may buy Gold too dear. If the SOUL be bartered away for Gold, verily, we buy Gold too dear! To get Riches and not by Right, is to render the SOUL obnoxious to the Wrath of GOD.

A SOUL perishing under the Wrath of GOD, is a Lost SOUL. Such is the SOUL of the Wicked, & of him who in Ill Wayes does make Haste to be Rich. No man can Wrong another man, but it may be said of him, He wrongs his own SOUL. A very Unjust man had it said unto him; Hab. II. 9, 10.

Wo to him that Coveteth an Evil Covetousness; Thou hast Sinned against thy SOUL. To Lose the1 pagecomes at the End of an Unjust Life; This, This will discover the Matchless Folly of all that is not Honestly done in and for the Getting of Riches.

They that Get Riches and not by Right, must know, that this Trade won't Last always. Their Way, & their Life, must come to an End. It won't be Long before they have such Tidings bro't unto them; Ezek VII. 6.

An End is come, the End is come, it watcheth for thee, behold, it is come! No Riches will keep any man always alive. 'Tis no New Thing, to have it said, The Rich man died. It is an Occurrence of daily Experience, That they who boast themselves in the multitude of their Riches, cannot Redeem a Brother, no, nor themselves, to Live forever, and not see Corruption.

Verily, The Fat Ones of the Earth cannot keep alive their own Souls. Much less, will the Mammon of Unrighteousness, keep off the Arrest of Death. But now, at the Death of the man who gets Riches and not by Right, What will there be Observable? Something to be Observed, by which the Folly shall be manifest unto all men. Come, Let us Mark the Unjust man, and behold the False Dealer, for the End of that man, will declare him to be a Fool.

First. There is oftentimes, an Early Death, in the Strange Punishment for these Workers of Iniquity. They that Get Riches, and not by Right, are oftentimes thus Punished; They must Leave them in the midst of their Days. Thus, we find a Rich Fool promising himself Goods Laid up for many years. But, in the midst of his Days he feels this Order from Heaven served upon him; Luke XII. 20.

Thou Fool, This night thy Soul shall be required of thee; Then whose shall these things be, which thou hast provided: The man must not Live to Taste the Sweet of his Ill-gotten Goods. And perhaps the Wealth of the Sinner, is Left unto a man more Just than himself. GOD required His People to deal Righteously with one another, and Employed this motive; Deut. XXV. 15.

That thy Days may be lengthened in the Land, which the Lord thy GOD giveth thee. But in Unrighteous Dealings, men take the most Ready Course, that their Dayes may be Shortened in the Land.

It is especially thus, when men grow more Dangerous Criminals, and are so sharp set with the Cursed Hunger of Riches, that they do things wherein Humane Society shall be considerably Damnified. Our Gracious GOD has a Wondrous Tenderness for Humane Society; And when men grow so Outrageous in the Ways of Dishonesty, that Humane Society suffers Insupportable Damages from them; Now there goes up that Cry to Heaven, 'Tis Time, Lord, for thee to Work! And, GOD comes down, GOD steps in, GOD in Compassion to Humane Society, fulfils that word upon the man who trusted in the abundance of his Riches, and Strengthened himself in his Wickedness; Psal. LII. 5.

GOD shall take thee away, and plack thee out of thy Dwelling-place, and Root thee out of the Land of the Living. Such Dangerous Criminals are Wicked overmuch. And the Doom of them that are Wicked overmuch, is, To Dy before their Time. Such Dangerous Criminals are Left sometimes to do Bloody as well as Deceitful Things.

And the Doom of such Bloody and Deceitful men, is, They shall not Live out half their Dayes. Yea, many times the Wretches run into Capital Crimes. It is reckoned among the Crimes of them who are Greedy of Gain; Prov. I. 15.

Their feet run to Evil, and make Haste to shed Blood. The Sword which is to defend Humane Society, now animadverts upon them. That Sword of GOD cuts them off. They Dy at the Place of Execution, and as a Fool dieth. O dismal Sight!

Young men drawn to the Place of Execution! Young men, who must flee to the Pit, and none may stay them! Young men, hurried out of the World, for having forfeited their Lives, by Getting Riches, and not by Right. Such a Sight is this Day to be seen among us; Behold, All ye your selves have seen it!

Secondly, But let the Death of the Wicked come when it will, be sure it Scribs them of all the Riches they were Possessed of. The Riches which have been gotten, and not by Right, many times Leave men before they Dy. There is a secret Blast from GOD, upon the Estates that have not been Honestly come at. GOD has many Ways to blist Ill-gotten Estates, and make such Treasures of to melt away to . Yea, Sometimes, if a man do but get a Little unrighteously, it proves a Moth to all the rest that he has gotten, and brings a strange Consumption upon it. But whether this fall out or no; This you may be certain of: When men Dy, then they must Leave all that they have got. So we are told, 1 Tim. VI 7.

We brought nothing into the World, and it is certain we can carry nothing out. Ah, Dying Man, Thou art going, thou art going from all thy Possessions: When thou Dyest, thou shalt carry nothing away, neither shall thy Glory descend after thee!

Thirdly. At the Death of men, and at the End of all, it will be found, That SIN is what nothing is to be gotten by! To Sin, 'Tis to do a Deceitful Work. O the Deceitfulness of Sin! Men dream of Getting, I know not what, by Sinning against the Blessed GOD. But, Be not Deceived: In the End it will be found, That nothing is to be Gotten, by the Unfruitful Works of Darkness. Men may for a while Hatter themselves, that Sin will bring small Gain unto the Crafts men; But Syrs, I will call upon you, as the Prophet of old upon a Deceived People; What will ye do in the end thereof? We read; Prov. X•. 21.

An inheritance may be gotten hastily at the beginning: But the End thereof shall not blessed. Be sure, it will be found so, a Dying Hour, and at that which will the End of all men At the End of Life, and when the Wickedness of the Wicked is brought unto an End; Then will be found, That nothing has been by Sinning, but only this, That Blessings of GOD have been all Sinned away. It is a Quaestion may many an Unrighteous Dealer into Agony; What is the Hope of the , tho' he hath Gained never so much, then GOD shall take away his Soul? Yea, All sorts of Impieties have this in them, to terrify you from committing of them. 'Tis a smart Interrogatory; & you will ill in the End have it put unto ; What Fruit have you had of these things, whereof you are now ashamed! For the End of those things is Death. What fruit will the Unchrist have, of his Lewdness? The End Death. All that he Gets is, shalt the Last. What Fruit will the have of his Tipling? The is Death. all that he Gets is, the , it bites like a , stings like an Adder. What ? What Gott?—Be thy Evil Ways what they will, O man, if thou Sin, and pervert that which it, Right, in the End thou shalt say, has not profited me! So in the End, the Sinner is a Fool!

After Admonitions from GOD SAVIOUR, if hope, there are ••ctions. Piety, that will find Reception with you.

First. It is to be hoped, That if any of you have Riches, and not by Right; you will it, it; Seek a Reconciliation with GOD; And come to that E•solution; Job XXX••. ••. If I have done Iniquity, I will do it no .

Secondly. It to be hoped, That you will all keep close to the Wayes of Unspotted Honesty; Be Harmless; Be Blameless; Offer to no man the least Injury in the World; Aim at the Benefit of others as well as your own: Prefer the Little of Righteous man, before the Treasures, of many Wicked. And be within the reach of that Consolation, Psal. CVI. 3.

Blessed is he who doth Righteousness at all times.

Thirdly. It is to be hoped, That instead of grasping inordinately after the Riches of this World, you will seek more importunately after the Durable Riches of the Spiritual Blessings in the Heavenly Places. Yea, Seek these True Riches an Holy Violence; Take them by ! Be in Earnest for the Riches of CHRIST, and for that Wisdom, the Merchandise whereof is better than the Merchandise of Silver, and the Gain thereof than Gold. Oh! Be Earnest for what you have set before you, in Eph. I. 18.

The Riches of the Glory of the Inheritance among the Saints.

FINIS.

Appendix

The Substance of the Examinations of John Brown, &c. Taken by Order of His Excellency the GOVERNOUR, on Monday the 6th of May, 1717.

JOhn Brown being interrogated saith, That he was born in the Island of Jamaica, is 25 Years old, and Unmarried. About a Year ago he belonged to a Ship Commanded by Capt. Kingston, which in her Voyage with Logwood to Holland was taken to the Leeward of the Havana by two Piratical Sloops, one Commanded by Hornygold and the other by a Frenchman called Labous, each having 70 Men on Board. The Pirates kept the Ship about 8 or 10 Days and then having taken out of her what they thought proper delivered her back to some of the Men, who belonged to her Labous kept the Examinate on board his Sloop about 4 Months, the English Sloop under Hornygolds command keeping company with them all that time.

Off Cape Corante they took two Spanish Briganteens without any resistance laden with Cocoa from Maraca. The Spaniards not coming up to the Pirates demand about the ransom were put a-shore and their Briganteens burn'd. They Sailed next to the Isle of Pines, where meeting with 3 or 4 English Sloops empty, they made use of them in cleaning their own, and gave them back. From thence they Sailed to Hispaniola in the latter end of May, where they tarryed about 3 Months.

The Examinate then left Labous and went on board the Sloop Commanded formerly by Hornygold, at that time by one Bellamy, who upon a difference arising amongst the English Pirates because Hornygold refused to take and plunder English Vessels, was chosen by a great Majority their Captain & Hornygold departed with 26 hands in a prize Sloop, Bellamy having then on Board about •• Men, most of them English Bellamy and Labous sailed to the Virgin Islands, and took several small Fishing Boats and off St Croix a French Ship laden with Flower and Fish from Canada, and having taken out some of the Flower gave back the Ship. Plying to the Windward the Morning they made Saba they spy'd 2 Ships, which they chased and came up with, one was Commanded by Capt. Richards, the other by Capt. Tosor both bound to the Bay.

Having plundered the Ships and taken out some Young Men they dismist the rest & likewise T•sor's Ship, and made a Man of War of Richard's, which they put under the Command of Bellamy, and appointed Paul Williams Captain of their Sloop. Next Day they took a Bristol Ship, Commanded by James Williams from Ireland laden with Provisions, and having taken out what Provisions they wanted and 2 or 3 of the Crew, let her go. They parted with their French consort at the Island of Blanco and stood away with their Ship and Sloop to the Windward passage, where in the latter end of February last they met with Capt. Lawrence Prince in a Ship of 300 Ton called the Whido with 18 Guns mounted, and 50 Men bound from Jamaica to London laden with Sugar, Indigo, Jesuits Bark and some Silver and Gold, and having given chase 3 Days took him without any other resistance than his firing two chase Guns at their Sloop, & came to an Anchor at Long Island.

Bellamy's crew and Williams's consisted then of 120 Men. They gave the Ship taken from Capt. Richards to Capt. Prince, and loaded her with as much of the best and finest goods as She could carry, and gave Capt. Prince above Twenty Pounds in Silver and Gold to bear his charges. They took 8 or 10 Men belonging to Capt. Prince, the Boatswain and two more were forced, the rest being Volunteers. Off Pettiguavis they took an English Ship hired by the French laden with Sugar and Indigo, and having taken out what they had occasion for, and some of the Map, dismist her.

Then they stood away for the Capes of Virginia, being 130 Men in company, and having lost sight of their Sloop the Day before they made the Land, they cruised ten Days according to agreement between Bellamy and Williams, in which time they seized 3 Ships and one Snow, two of them from Scotland, one from Bristol, and the fourth a Scotch Ship from Barbadoes with a little Rum and Sugar on Board, so leaky that the Men refused to proceed farther. The Pirates sunk her. Having lost the Sloop they kept the Snow, which was taken from one Montgomery, being about 100 Ton and manned her with 18 hands, which with her own Crew made up the number of 28 Men; the other 2 Ships were discharged being first plundered.

They made the best of their way for Cape Cod intending to clean their Ship at Green Island (having one. & an Indian born at Cape Cod for Pilots) and on Friday the 26th of April last to the Eastward of Cape Cod took a Pink laden with Wine from Madera, last from Boston, bound to New York. They sent seven Men on Board called out on the Watch Bill, of whom the Examinate was one. He further saith, that there were about 50 Men forced, over whom the Pirates kept a watchful eye, and no Man was suffered to write a word, but what was Nailed up to the Mast.

The names of the forced Men were put in the watch Bill and fared as others, they might have had what Money they wanted from the Quarter Master, who kept a Book for that purpose, but this Examinate took only Cloaths. It was the common report in their Ship, that they had about 20000 Pounds in Gold and Silver. That Peter Hoof was once whip'd for attempting to Run-away, and that he and every one of the other Prisoners were forced to Join the Pirates

THomas Baker being Examined saith, That he was Born in Flushing, Aged 29 Years, by Trade a Taylor, and sometimes went to Sea, and sometimes followed his Trade ashore That he was taken with 9 more in a little Boat coming from Cape Francois, by Bellamy and Labous, but they were sent away being Married Men. This Examinate was never sworn as the rest were. Being on Board of Lebous he asked leave to go on Board of Bellamy, that he might have an opportunity of getting away, and accordingly he went, but found that Bellamy would not discharge him, on the contrary threatned to set him ashore on a Moroon Island if he would not be easy.

When they took Richards, Tosor and Williams they spread a large black Flag, with a Death's Head and Bones a-cross, and gave chase to Captain Prince under the same Colours. They had on Board 20000 or 30000 Pounds, and the Quarter Master declared to the Company, that if any Man wanted Money he might have it. The Examinate came on Board the Pink which was taken off Cape Cod, Armed. The reason why he and the other Prisoners did not discover themselves to the Government when they first came ashore was because they expected to get to Boston and there Ship themselves as Sailors. In all other particulars he agrees with what is above.

THomas Davis Examined saith, He was born in Carmarthenshire in Wales, Aged Two & twenty Years, is by Trade a Ship wright, and has used the Sea these five Years. He Sail'd from Bristol with Capt. Williams, and was taken on the 19th of December last, by 9 leagues to the Leeward of Blanco, and in January he joyned Bellamy's company. When the company was called together to Consuls, and each Man to give his Vote, they would not allow the forced Men to have a Vote. There were One hundred and thirty forced Men in all, and Eighty of the Old company; and this Examinate being a forced Man had no opportunity to discover his Mind. From Blance they Sail'd to the Spanish Main and water'd there, and from thence to a Moroon Island called Testegos, where they fitted up a Ship and Sloop of their own.

All the New Men were Sworn to be true and not to cheat the company to the value of a piece of Eight. That when they chased the Whido they thought they had lost her but came up with her the third day. Capt. Prince was treated civily. What Money they got in the Whido was not shared. Seven or eight of the Whido's Crew joyned them. That their design in coming on this Coast was to get Provisions: That three of the Vessels, they look off the Capes of Virginia, belonged to Scotland, and the fourth to Bredhampston, and when a Prize was taken the Watch bill was called over, and Men put on board as they stood named in the Bill, and no more imposed on the forced Men than the Volunteers, they being all alike.

The same day the Whido was lost, they took a Sloop coming from Virginia. The Ship being at an Anchor, they cut their Cables and ran a shoar, in a quarter of an hour after the Ship struck, the Main-mast was carried by the board, and in the Morning She was beat to pieces. About Sixteen Prisoners drown'd, Crumpstey Master of the Pink being one, and One hundred and forty-four in all. The riches on board were laid together in one heap.

PEter Hooff declares, That he was born in Sweden, is about 34 Years old, and left his Country 18 Years ago. He Sail'd for the most part with the Dutch on the Coast of Portobello, and has been with the Pirates fourteen Months When he was taken by Bellamy in a Persaga, he belong'd to a Ship whereof one Cornelison was Master: Three Weeks after he was taken they went to Portobello in a French Sloop with 60 Men on board; then stood for the Havana, and from thence to Cuba, where they met with a Pink, an English-man Master, and took out some Powder and Shot, and some Men.

A difference arising amongst them about taking Prisoners; Some being for one Nation and some for another; and having at that time Two Sloops and about 100 Men, Hornygold parted from them in One of the Sloops, and Bellamy and Labous kept company together. They turned to the Windward from the Isle of Pines to look out for a Ship of Force.

The Money taken in the Whido, which was reported to Amount to 20000 or 30000 Pounds, was counted over in the Cabin, and put up in bags, Fifty Pounds to every Man's share, there being 180 Men on Board. No Married Men were forced. Their Money was kept in Chests between Decks without any guard, but none was to take any without the Quarter Masters leave.

JOhn Shuan declares, That he was born in Nantes, 24 Years old, a Mariner. That Two Months and an half ago he was taken by Bellamy in an English Ship coming from Jamaica, commanded by an English-man, and a French-man, bound from Pettiguavis to Rochel, with Sugar. This Examinate knows nothing of the Scotch Vessel's being sunk. When Crumpstey's Pink was taken on this Coast, He desired Bellamy to give him leave to go on board her, but could not obtain it, by reason he had not taken up Arms, yet afterwards Bellamy let him go. He further declares, That he never was upon the List as the rest were: That in the Ship he belong'd to the Pirates found 5000 Liyres, and on board of Bellamy's there was a great quantity of Silver and Gold.

SImon Van Vorst declares, That he was born in the City of New-York, aged 24 Years. That he went from New-York to St. Thomas's, and from thence to Cape Francois, where he staid three Months, and came from thence in October last in a Boat with Captain Simsons Men, who were Prisoners there,

APPENDIX

and standing over to Cape Nicholas they spy'd two Sail, which came pretty near them, and firing a Gun brought them on board, three were dismist, being Married. The Examinate desired Labous to let him goe on board of Bellamy, and accordingly he went, Bellamy told him he must be easy until they could find Volunteers, or he would put him a shoar on some Moroon Island.

Next day they took a Sloop coming from Cape Francois, and soon after a French Ship, out of which they took Claret and Provisions. They cleaned at St. Croix, where 3 of their Men Ran away, and one of them being brought back was severely whipped. Plying to Windward for what they could get they took Richards, Tosor and a Bristol Ship laden with Beef. He further declares, That he saw many of Williams's, Tosor's and Richards's Men Cry & express their Grief upon their being compelled to go with Bellamy. After the Whido was taken they gave Richards's Ship to Capt. Prince and put as great a quantity of Goods on Board, as he desired. They took 10 or 12 of Prince's Men of whom the Boatswain and 2 or 3 more were forced. The Examinate went on Board Crumpsty's Pink Armed with a Gun and Pistol, and he and the other 6, who were with him were all equal as to the commanding part, being in course according to the list or Watch Bill.

HEndrick Quintor declares, He was born in Amsterdam, Aged 25 Years, a Mariner. That he was taken in a Spanish Briganteen by Labous Commander of the Sloop *Postillion,* and Bellamy Commander of the Sloop Mary Anne and being bound to , the Pirates told him he should go to the Coast of Crocus, but afterwards they compelled him to stay, and during the time he was with them they took 3 French Ships and then clean'd at the Main Land of Hispaniola. After that they took 3 English Ships, viz. Richards's, Tosor's and Williams's, and went to the Main to Water, from thence to Testegos, the Wind blowing very hard they went to St Croix, where a French Pirate was blown up. That this Examinate and the other six, who were sent on Board the Pink were Forced Men.

THomas South saith, He was born in Boston in Lincolnshire, about 30 Years of Age, a Mariner. That he came from Cork in Ireland in a Ship Commanded by Capt. Williams bound to Jamaica, and was taken by the Pirate Bellamy about four Months ago. The Pirates forced such as were Unmarried, being four in number two of them were drown'd in the Whido, a Dutchman and a Welshman. This Examinate further saith, That the Pirates brought Arms to him, but he told them, He would not use any, for which he was much threatned; they staid sometime at Spanish To••; when Captain Richards's Ship was taken this Examinate did not take up Arms, he only stood by the Rigging. That they came on this Coast to meet their consort Paul Williams, whom they expected to find at Block Island That he was One of Seven, who were sent on board the Pink, He told the Mate that he was a forced Man, and if he could get a-shoar he would run away. And further declares, That he has heard the other Prisoners say, They were compelled to joyn the Pirates.

FINIS.

The Reader is desired to Correct with his Pen the following Errors.

PAge 1. line 3. read Eighteenth. p. 2. l. 15. r. Reign. p. 8. l. 10. r.. p. 11. l. 11. say Brown r. Baker. p. 12. l. 19. for Thomas r. John. p. 17. l. 22. r. aggravating. p. 29. l. 51. r. Firm and Seal. p. 21. l. 16. r. confinement nor restraint. p. 22. l. 32. r. had ever prevail'd. For Indictment r. Inditement throughout.

Bibliography

Alden, Timothy. *A Collection of American Epitaphs and Inscriptions with Occasional Notes* Volume IV. S. Marks, 1814.

Brooks, Baylus C. *Quest for Blackbeard: The True Story of Edward Thache and His World*, Lulu Press, Inc., 2016

Burgess, Robert F. *Finding Sunken Treasure: True Story of the Pirate Ship Whydah.* Spyglass Publications, 2012.

Carpenter, John Reeve. *Pirates: Scourge of the Seas.*Barnes & Noble, 2006.

Carpenter, John Reeve. *Pirates: Scourge of the Seas*. Gusto Company AS for Barnes & Noble, New York, 2006

Carr, John Laurence. *Life in France under Louis XIV.*B.T. Batsford, 1970.

Clifford, Barry, and Kenneth J. Kinkor with Sharon Simpson. *Real Pirates: The Untold Story of the Whydah from Slave Ship to Pirate Ship*. National Geographic, 2007.

Clifford, Barry with Paul Perry. *Expedition Whydah: The Story of the World's First Excavation of a Pirate Treasure Ship and the Man Who Found Her*. Cliff Street Books, 1999.

Cordingly, David. *Under the Black Flag: The Romance and the Reality of Life Among the Pirates*. Random House, 2006.

Dampier, William. *A New Voyage Round the World*. Printed for James Knapton at the Crown in St. Paul's Churchyard, MDCXCIX

Dana, Richard Henry. *Two Years Before the Mast*. Penguin Books, 1840.

Defoe, Daniel. *A General History of the Pyrates*. Edited by Manual Schonhorn. Dover, 1972.

Dethlefsen, Edwin. *Whidah: Cape Cod's Mystery Treasure Ship.* Seafarer's Heritage Library, 1984.

Donovan, Webster. "Pirates of the Whydah." *National Geographic Magazine* (May 1999).

"Examination of Jeremiah Higgins" New York, 22 June 1717. *Records of the Vice-Admiralty Court of the Province of New York 1685-1838*, 36-3.

Friedenberg, Zachary B. *Medicine Under Sail.* Naval Institute Press, Annapolis, MD, 2002.

Jugement du Pirate La Buse, du 7 Juillet 1730. Archives departementales de la Reunion, Serie C, Registredu greffe du Counseil Superieur de Bourbon siegeant au judiciare.

Kinkor, Kenneth J. "Black Men Under the Black Flag. "In *Bandits At Sea: A Pirate Reader* edited by C. R. Pennell. New York University, 2001.

Lee, Robert E. *Blackbeard the Pirate: A Reappraisal of His Life and Times.* John F. Blair, 1974.

Levenson, Michael. "Remains Are Identified as a Boy Pirate." *Boston Globe*, 2 June 2006.

Lost Treasure Magazine, April 2015, pp. 53-54.

Mather, Cotton. "Instructions to the Living, from the Condition of the Dead." in *British Piracy in the Golden Age* edited by Joel H. Baer. Pickering & Chatto, 2007, 4:129-144.

Mather, Cotton. *"Warnings to Them that Make Haste to be Rich"* in *British Piracy in the Golden Age* edited by Joel H. Baer. Pickering & Chatto, 2007, 4: 145–153.

Maugh, Thomas H. *"A Pirate's Life for Him – at Age 9."* *Los Angeles Times.* 1 June 2006.

Moisan, Elizabeth. *Master of the Sweet Trade: A Story of the Pirate Samuel Bellamy, Mariah Hallett, and the Whydah.* iUniverse, 2009.

Rediker, Marcus. *Villains of All Nations: Atlantic Pirates in the Golden Age.* Beacon Press, 2005.

Reynard, Elizabeth. "The 'Pyrats' and the Posse," in *The Narrow Land: Folk Chronicles of Old Cape Cod.* Chatham Historical Society, 1993.

Rogers, Mary Bangs. "Storms and Pirates." *Old Cape Cod: The Land, the*

Men, the Sea. Houghton Mifflin, 1931

Skinner, Charles M. "The Wild Man of Cape Cod." *Myths and Legends of Our Own Land*, Volume 1. JB Lippincott, 1896.

Snow, Edward Rowe. *Boston Sunday Post* (28 September 1947).

Swift, Charles F. "The Cape in the Old French Wars."*Cape Cod the Right Arm of Massachusetts; A Historical Narrative*. Register Publishing, 1897.

Thoreau, Henry David. *Cape Cod*. Parnassus, 1984.

"The Trials of Eight Persons Indited [sic] for Piracy, *"British Piracy in the Golden Age*, edited by Joel H. Baer, (2: 289-319). Pickering and Chatto, 2007.

"Understanding Stockholm Syndrome" by Nathalie de Fabrique, Stephen J. Romano, Gregory M. Vecchi, and Vincent B. Van Hasselt in the July 2007 FBI Law Enforcement Bulletin, US Dept of Justice, FBI, 76:7, 10-15.

Vallar, Cindy. *"Cotton Mather, Preacher to the Pirates."* At *Pirates & Privateers*, on her *Thistles and Pirates* web site.

Vanderbilt, Arthur T. *Treasure Wreck: The Fortunes and Fate of the Pirate Ship Whydah*. Schiffler Publishing, 2007.

Woodard, Colin. *"Black Flags Down East,"* Down East, the Magazine of Maine* 54:1, August, 2007.

Woodard, Colin. *The Republic of Pirates: Being the True and Surprising Story of the Caribbean Pirates and the Man Who Brought Them Down*. Harcourt, 2007.

Index

Adams, President John Quincy, 39, 41
 Anne Galley, 63
 Antigua, 58, 63, 68
Auchmuty, Robert, 25, 86, 87, 90
Baker, Thomas, 21, 23, 29, 38, 47, 79, 82, 83, 84, 85, 86, 89, 103, 104, 106, 107, 110, 113, 114, 115, 140, 146, 152, 154, 155, 156, 161, 176, 177
Barbados, 118, 139
Barnstable Gaol, 20, 47
Bay of Honduras, 26, 35
Baya Honda, 16, 36
Bellamy, Samuel, 2, 7, 11, 15, 16, 17, 18, 25, 33, 35, 36, 43, 44, 45, 47, 48, 51, 52, 53, 54, 55, 56, 57, 58, 59, 62, 63, 67, 68, 69, 71, 72, 73, 102, 103, 104, 106, 107, 108, 109, 110, 111, 112, 125, 126, 127, 128, 129, 131, 132, 138, 139, 140, 141, 142, 143, 144, 145,146, 151, 198, 205
Benjamin, 11, 16, 24, 51, 52, 80
Blackbeard, 16, 22, 26, 36, 54, 63, 197, 198
Blackett, 52
Block Island, 62, 146
Bonetta, 57, 58, 67
Boston Gaol, 21, 38, 42, 47, 60, 61, 91, 105, 127
Boston, Massachusetts, 13, 21, 22, 23, 26, 30, 38, 42, 45, 47, 49, 50, 53, 73, 79, 80, 82, 88, 89, 116, 120, 127, 140, 141, 146, 149, 152, 153, 198, 199
Brett, John, 107, 108, 126, 129, 131

INDEX

Bristol, 109, 125, 128, 130, 138, 139, 141, 144

Brown, John, 13, 15, 18, 21, 23, 29, 38, 47, 53, 58, 79, 82, 83, 84, 85, 86, 89, 104, 105, 107, 108, 109, 113, 114, 115, 137, 146, 152, 162, 177

Cape Cod, 9, 19, 30, 33, 37, 38, 43, 44, 47, 48, 50, 51, 58, 59, 68, 72, 73, 104, 140, 141, 197, 198, 199

Cape Corrientes, 16, 36

Cape Nicholas, 16, 144

Carmarthenshire, Wales, 141

Checkley, Thomas, 42, 108, 112

Christophers, Joseph, 61

Clifford, Barry, 9, 69

Cole, John, 19, 105, 108

Condent, Christopher, 36

Cornelison, John, 25

Corney, John, 130

Crab Island, 110

Crumpstey, Andrew, 24, 37, 45, 74, 84, 102, 103, 106, 142, 143, 144

Damariscove, 61

Dampier, William, 11, 34

Davis, Howell, 36

Davis, Thomas, 21, 25, 33, 37, 38, 43, 45, 47, 73, 79, 91, 116, 117, 118, 119, 120, 126, 136, 141

de Bry, John, 69

De Lorme, 57

Dispatch, 61

Doane, Joseph, 19, 20, 105, 109

Dunavan, James, 103, 106

Eastham Tavern, 109

Eastham, Massachusetts, 19, 20, 43, 49, 72, 105, 108, 151

England, Edward, 36

Fisher, 37, 43, 73

Fitzgerald, Thomas, 18, 19, 102, 114

Fletcher, John, 52

Fox, Thomas, 127, 132
French, John, 130
Frost, Captain, 59, 60, 61
Glyn, Thomas, 127, 128, 129
Green, Bartholomew, 79
Haiti, 16, 36
Hallett, Maria, 43, 72
Hamilton, Governor Walter, 63, 68
Harding, Samuel, 38
Higgins, Jeremiah, 51, 53, 198
Hoof, Peter Cornelius, 2, 5, 7, 9, 10, 11, 12, 13, 14, 15, 16, 17, 19, 21, 22, 23, 25, 26, 27, 29, 30, 31, 38, 44, 47, 72, 79, 82, 83, 84, 85, 86, 89, 110, 113, 114, 115, 140, 142, 153, 165, 176
Hornigold, Benjamin, 11, 16, 51, 52, 53, 54, 138, 143
Hornygold. *See* Hornigold, Benjamin
Hume, Captain Frances, 64
Hunt, David, 69
Isle of Pines, 16, 36, 55, 108, 137, 143
Jamaica, 52, 58, 68, 114, 117, 125, 128, 130, 137, 138, 143, 146, 152
Julian, John, 2, 7, 21, 33, 38, 39, 40, 43, 47, 128
King George, 22, 104
King, John, 2, 7, 57, 58, 63, 67, 68, 69, 70, 74, 75
Kinkor, Kenneth J, 35, 69, 198
La Buse. *See* Levasseur, Olivier
La Isla Blanquilla, 36
Labous. *See* Levasseur, Olivier
Lamb, Abraham, 52
Leeward Islands, 63
Levasseur, Olivier, 2, 5, 7, 11, 36, 51, 53, 54, 55, 56, 57, 58, 59, 60, 61, 62, 63, 64, 65, 107, 108, 110, 111, 112, 128, 137, 138, 140, 143, 144, 145
Lucy, Peter, 88
Machias, Maine, 62Mackconacky, Alexander, 47, 103, 104, 105, 106, 107
Main, Mr., 59, 60

INDEX

Marconi Beach, 38, 46

Marshal, Vincent, 115

Mary Anne, 17, 18, 23, 24, 37, 38, 43, 47, 51, 52, 53, 57, 62, 63, 68, 84, 102, 106, 107, 109, 110, 114, 145

Mather, Reverend Cotton, 23, 27, 147, 199

Matinicus, 61

Middle Passage, 17

Moisan, Elizabeth, 42

Monhegan, 61, 62

Morris, Isaac, 127

Morris, Owen, 125, 129, 131

Nassau, 59, 62, 63, 64

New England, 44, 59, 61, 63, 73, 89, 116, 127

Noland, Richard, 63

Norman, Moses, 108

Noyes, Oliver, 129

Old State House, 30

Osgood, Peter, 130

Ouidah, 33

Portobello, 11, 36, 142

Portsmouth, New Hampshire, 59

Postillion, 53, 57, 68, 145

Prince, Captain Lawrence, 17, 71, 117, 125, 131, 138, 139, 142, 144

Protestant Caesar, 26

Provincetown Harbor, 48

Provincetown, Massachusetts, 9

Puerto Rico, 16, 36, 56

Quincy, John, 39, 41

Quintor, Hendrick, 21, 23, 38, 47, 79, 82, 83, 84, 85, 86, 89, 110, 113, 114, 115, 145, 153, 169

Real Pirates Exhibit, 9

Reunion Island, 64

Rhode Island, 21, 43, 72, 105, 108, 109

Richards, John, 58, 125, 126, 128, 129, 138, 139, 141, 144, 145, 146
Roberts, Bart, 35, 36
Rogers, Woodes, 64
Rose, Captain, 63
Samana Bay, 16
Savage, Abijah, 57, 68
Seaford, 63
Shrimpton, Samuel, 130
Shuan, John, 21, 23, 38, 47, 79, 82, 83, 84, 85, 86, 88, 89, 102, 105, 106, 107, 108, 110, 111, 112, 113, 114, 115, 143, 153, 171, 172, 173, 174
Shute, Samuel, 23, 80, 89, 116, 120
Smith, Seth, 127
Smith, William, 105
South, Thomas, 17, 21, 23, 26, 38, 47, 79, 82, 83, 84, 85, 86, 89, 102, 104, 106, 107, 109, 111, 112, 114, 115, 126, 129, 132, 146, 153
Spanish Town, 110
St. Croix, 13, 17, 36, 56, 70, 144
St. Michael, 125, 126, 128
St. Thomas, 63, 144
Sultana Galley, 17, 58, 59, 71, 125, 126, 131
Teach, Edward, 16, 54
Valentine, John, 119, 120, 128, 130
Van Vorst, Simon, 13, 21, 25, 38, 47, 79, 82, 83, 84, 85, 86, 89, 104, 106, 107, 109, 110, 113, 114, 115, 144, 152, 156, 177
Virginia, 59, 103, 118, 126, 131, 139, 142
Wellfleet, Massachusetts, 47, 48
Whidaw. See Whydah Galley
Whido. See Whydah Galley
Whydah Galley, 1, 5, 9, 10, 12, 13, 17, 18, 22, 23, 24, 25, 29, 30, 33, 37, 38, 39, 43, 44, 45, 47, 58, 59, 69, 71, 72, 73, 74, 77, 85, 100, 102, 103, 106, 107, 109, 111, 114, 117, 125, 126, 128, 131, 133, 136, 138, 142, 143, 144, 146, 149, 151, 152, 197, 198, 199
Williams, James, 109, 125, 126, 128, 138, 141, 144, 145, 146

INDEX

Williams, Paulsgrave, 58, 62, 63, 125, 138, 139, 146
Woodard, Colin, 35

Notes

PETER CORNELIUS HOOF AND ME

1. Real Pirates tells the story of the *Whydah* (whih-duh)and how she went from being a slave ship to a pirate ship. It's a traveling exhibit sponsored by National Geographic with artifacts from the *Whydah* Pirate Museum in Provincetown, Massachusetts and established by Barry Clifford, the underwater explorer who discovered the wreck of the *Whydah* off Cape Cod.
2. Peter Hoof is not the lover that is mentioned here. That person's name is Andre.
3. A periaga, more commonly spelled piragua or pirogue,was a canoe favored by Caribbean pirates during the seventeenth and eighteenth centuries. Both Alexandre Esquemelin and William Dampier described them in their books. Benerson Little provides more details on these favored boats in *A Sea Rover's Practice* on pages 49-52. Also *"The Trials of Eight Persons Indited for Piracy,"* p. 318.
4. Clifford, Barry. *Expedition Whydah*, p. 137.
5. *"The Trials of Eight Persons Indited for Piracy,"* p 318.
6. Ibid, p 319.
7. Friedenberg, Zachary B. *Medicine Under Sail*, p. 31. Appointed chief physician to the Haslar Naval Hospital in 1797, Thomas Trotter observed young patients who were despondent, "He attributed this to the horror of the patients whose next bed neighbor might be a seaman hospitalized because of brutal laceration and festering sores at the draining sites of whiplash wounds on his back and buttocks." The United States Navy did not abolish flogging until 1840.
8. *"The Trials of Eight Persons Indited for Piracy,"* p 319.
9. Ibid, p. 318
10. *"The Trials of Eight Persons Indited for Piracy,"* p 306.
    "Understanding Stockholm Syndrome" 10-15. Nowadays we call this phenomenon the Stockholm Syndrome, where hostages or captives identify with their captors and perhaps even to defend them. The name derives from a 1973 incident in Stockholm, Sweden. At the end of six days of captivity in a bank, several kidnap victims actually resisted rescue attempts and afterwards refused to testify against their captors. The behavior is considered a common survival strategy for victims of interpersonal abuse. Two of the most famous examples are Patty Hearst and more recently, Elizabeth Smart.
11. *"The Trials of Eight Persons Indited for Piracy,"* p 319.

NOTES

12 Ibid, p. 303

13 Ibid, p. 304

14 Ibid, p. 304

15 Eastham is on Cape Cod.

16 Lee, Robert E. *Blackbeard the Pirate*, p. 243

17 Cordingly, David. *Under the Black Flag*, p. 205

18 Woodard, Colin. *The Republic of Pirates*, p. 227

19 "*The Trials of Eight Persons Indited for Piracy*," p. 319

20 "*The Trials of Eight Persons Indited for Piracy*," p. 296

21 "*The Trials of Eight Persons Indited for Piracy*," p. 297

22 "*The Trials of Eight Persons Indited for Piracy*," p. 297

23 Ibid, p. 297

24 Ibid, p. 299

25 Ibid, p. 306

26 Mather, Cotton. "*Instructions to the Living, from the Condition of the Dead*," p. 143

27 Ibid, p. 143

JOHN JULIAN - THE TEENAGE PIRATE

28 "Whydah" (pronounced (whih-duh) derives from the African kingdom of Ouidah, which developed into a major center for the exportation of slaves. Located in the Republic of Benin, the Ouidah Museum of History introduces visitors to the town's history and involvement in the slave trade.

29 Clifford, Barry. *Real Pirates*, p. 81

30 Dampier, William. *A New Voyage Round the World*.p. 7-8

31 Ibid, p. 7. According to D. Smith's *A Voyage to Constantinople* (1668) the fisgig was "a kind of barbed iron at the end of a pole tyed fast to a rope." It was used to spear fish.

32 Ibid, p. 10

33 Woodard, Colin. *The Republic of Pirates*, p. 89 & 185. Based in the Bay of Honduras in March 1716 Bellamy and his men sailed aboard two periaguas. These canoes were "capable of carrying thirty men and an ample supply of cargo. Equipped with banks of oars and a single fore-and-aft rigged sail, they were well suited to small scale piracy: swift, able to row straight into the wind to catch or escape from a square-rigged vessel, and drawing so little water they could be rowed or sailed over shoals, coral heads, and other hazards to give would-be pursuers the slip." The periagua was often the first vessel pirates acquired; thereafter, they would capture bigger and bigger vessels.

34 Kinkor, Kenneth J. "Black Men Under the Black Flag," p. 204. Many pirate histories say the opposite of this statement. Kinkor disputes this. "Although seventy blacks were as active as any among Bart Roberts's crew, they were delivered to the Royal African Company in 1722 without trial.... In 1724 captured black pirates were likewise sold in lieu of trial. These were, however, minority opinions. In trial after trial, blacks were placed on the same legal footing as whites. They comprise an undetermined percentage of an estimated four hundred pirates executed during the decade 1716-1726. Most went silently to the gallows...."

35 Ibid, p. 200.

36 Clifford, Barry, *Real Pirates*, p. 130

37 Clifford, Barry, *Expedition Whydah*, p. 318. "An Arctic gale from Canada was colliding with a warm front moving north-west from the Caribbean. Their confluence produced one of the worst storms ever to strike Cape Cod."
Ibid, p. 262 "Technically known as an occluded front, the warm and moist tropical air is driven for miles upward where it cools and falls at a very high speed, producing high winds, heavy rain, and severe lightning."

38 Donovan Webster, *"Pirates of the Whydah"*

39 *"The Trials of Eight Persons Indited for Piracy,"* p. 318.

40 Clifford, Barry, *Expedition Whydah*, p. 318

41 Donovan Webster, *"Pirates of the Whydah"*

42 Clifford, Barry, *Real Pirates*, p. 131.

43 "John Julian – Only Free at Sea" at *"Pirates of the Whydah"*, National Geographic. In February 1839, John Quincy Adams successfully represented the slaves from the *Amistad* rebellion. More information about this case can be read at the National Archives web site.

44 Ibid.

45 "The Lives of Individual African Americans before 1783" at Massachusetts Historical Society.

46 Moisan, Elizabeth. *Master of the Sweet Trade.*

THE UNKNOWN SURVIVOR

47 Clifford, Barry, *Real Pirates*, p. 130.

48 *"The Trials of Eight Persons Indited for Piracy,"* p. 319.
Peter Cornelius Hoof said in his testimony: "The Money taken in the *Whido*, which was reported to amount to 20000 to 30000 Pounds, was counted over in the Cabin, and put up in bags, Fifty Pounds to every Man's share, there being 180 Men on Board... but none was to take any without the Quarter Masters leave."

49 Clifford, Barry, *Expedition Whydah*, p. 260. "Technically known as an occluded front, the warm and moist tropical air is driven for miles upward where it cools and falls at a very high speed, producing high winds, heavy rain, and severe lightning."

50 Donovan, Webster. *"Pirates of the Whydah."*

51 *"The Trials of Eight Persons Indited for Piracy,"* p. 318.

52 Clifford, Barry, *Real Pirates*, p. 131.

53 Donovan, Webster. *"Pirates of the Whydah."*

54 Thoreau, Henry David. *Cape Cod.* p. 186-187.

55 Snow, Edward Rowe. *Boston Sunday Post* (28 September 1947).

SAM BELLAMY & OLIVIER LEVASSEUR – TWO PIRATES JUST KICKIN' AROUND THE CARIBBEAN

56 *"Examination of Jeremiah Higgins"* 36-3.

57 *"The Trials of Eight Persons Indited for Piracy,"* p. 317.

58 When Hornigold sailed away, his supporters included a man named Edward Teach, soon to be known as Blackbeard.

59 My research has found Levasseur listed as: Oliver La Buse, Olivier Levasseur, Louis Lebous, M. Leboos, La Buze, La Bouze, Oliver La Bouche, Louis de Boure, and Louis La Buse.

60 Carr, John Laurence. *Life in France under Louis XIV*, p. 59.
   Jugement du Pirate La Buse
   In France at this time, bourgeois families educated their children at home by hiring private tutors. When they completed their education with the tutor, they might be sent to college, where instruction in religion was the most common field of study.

61 Clifford, Barry, *Real Pirates*, p. 55.

62 Ibid, p. 58.

63 Vanderbilt, Arthur T. *Treasure Wreck*, p. 23.

64 Clifford, Barry, *Real Pirates*, p. 132.

65 Dethlefsen, Edwin. *Whidah: Cape Cod's Mystery Treasure Ship*, p. 127 – 129.

66 Clifford, Barry, *Real Pirates*, p. 132. All three items are on display as part of National Geographic's *Real Pirates* traveling exhibit.

67 *"The Trials of Eight Persons Indited for Piracy,"* p. 317.

68 Defoe, Daniel. *A General History of the Pyrates.* p. 117. Most records don't mention him again until 1719, when Edward England found out that Levasseur had arrived at Whydah Road before him and "forestall'd the Market, and greatly disappointed their Brethren."

69 Woodard, Colin. *"Black Flags Down East,"* p. 116. At the time Levasseur separated from Bellamy, Bellamy was in command of the *Sultana*. Bellamy captured the *Whydah* in late February or early March, and this was the ship he commanded when she sank off Cape Cod.

70 Cordingly, David. *Under the Black Flag*, p. 120.

71 *Boston Newsletter*, 19 July 1717.
72 *Boston Newsletter*, 19 July 1717.
73 *Boston Newsletter*, 25 July 1717.
74 *BostonNewsletter*, 25 July 1717.
75 *Boston Newsletter*, 25 July 1717.
76 Woodard, Colin. "*Black Flags Down East*," p. 116.
77 Woodard, Colin. *The Republic of Pirates*, p. 321.
    Brooks, Baylus C. *Quest for Blackbeard*, p. 643.
    Williams would appear in historical accounts again in 1718 when he signed for the King's Pardon and again in 1720 as quartermaster of a ship commanded by Levasseur.
78 Woodard, Colin. *The Republic of Pirates*, p. 221.
79 Cordingly, David. *Under the Black Flag*.
    In a personal email from Cordingly to the author, Cordingly said that this reference came from a note by Geoffrey Callender (first Director of the National Maritime Museum, Greenwich) published in "The Mariner's Mirror," volume XXVII (1941) p. 264.

JOHN KING – THE BOY PIRATE

80 Carpenter, John Reeve. *Pirates: Scourge of the Seas*.
    A powder monkey was a boy who carried gunpowder from the ship's hold to the gun decks.
81 Clifford, Barry, *Real Pirates*, p. 132.
82 Dethlefsen, Edwin. *Whidah: Cape Cod's Mystery Treasure Ship*, p. 127 – 128.
83 Ibid, p. 129.
84 These items are on display as part of National Geographic's *Real Pirates* traveling exhibit.
85 Maugh, Thomas H. "*A Pirate's Life for Him – at Age 9.*"
    Los Angeles Times. 1 June 2006.
86 Ibid.
87 Ibid.
88 The cat-o'nine-tails consisted of a baton-like handle with nine rope or leather cords extending from it. The cords were often tipped with pieces of iron or steel hooks to inflict maximum damage. The usual rule amongst pirate crews was to follow the "Law of Moses" and give the person forty stripes.
89 Clifford, Barry, *Real Pirates*, p. 88.
90 Ibid, p. 130.
91 "*The Trials of Eight Persons Indited for Piracy*," p. 319.
    According to Peter Cornelius Hoof's testimony before his trial for piracy in 1717, "The money taken in the *Whido*, which was reported to amount to 20,000 to 30,000 pounds

[sterling] was counted over in the cabin, and put up in bags, fifty pounds to every man's share, there being 180 men on board."

92 Clifford, Barry, *Real Pirates*, p. 260.
93 Clifford, Barry, *Expedition Whydah*, p. 262. "Technically known as an occluded front, the warm and moist tropical air is driven for miles upward where it cools and falls at a very high speed, producing high winds, heavy rain, and severe lightning."
94 Donovan, Webster. "Pirates of the Whydah."
95 *"The Trials of Eight Persons Indited for Piracy,"* p. 318.
96 Clifford, Barry, *Real Pirates*, p. 131.
97 Donovan, Webster. "Pirates of the Whydah."

About the Author

I am a graduate of Augustana College in Rock Island, Ill. I am also a certified Paralegal. When not researching, reading, or writing about pirates, I enjoy walking, cats, and Tai Chi, to name a few. I now live in Cochiti Lake, New Mexico.

You can connect with me on:

🌐 https://petercorneliushoof.blogspot.com

📘 https://www.facebook.com/TheWhydahPiratesSpeak;%20https://www.facebook.com/LouisLaBuse;%20and%20https://www.facebook.com/PeterCorneliusHoof

Also by Laura Nelson

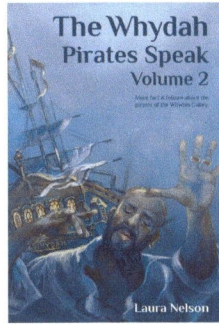

The Whydah Pirates Speak, Volume 2
This is my second collection of non-fiction articles about the pirates of the Whydah Galley. Sail with Sam Bellamy and relive the adventures and the dangers of life as a pirate in the Golden Age of Piracy.

www.ingramcontent.com/pod-product-compliance
Lightning Source LLC
Chambersburg PA
CBHW040459240426
43662CB00047B/64